building of The Mother Church

The First Church of Christ, Scientist
in Boston, Massachusetts

building of The Mother Church

The First Church of Christ, Scientist
in Boston, Massachusetts

Joseph Armstrong

Margaret Williamson

*the christian science
publishing society*

boston, massachusetts

This book combines *The Mother Church* by Joseph Armstrong and
The Mother Church Extension by Margaret Williamson. New photographs
and a brief third section have been added.

Design and typography by David Ford

contents

The Portico

illustrations

foreword

This volume tells the story of church building and dedication. More than that, it illustrates, in the very process of construction, spiritual healing—the basic purpose of the Church of Christ, Scientist.

The interest in spiritual healing as taught and preached by Mary Baker Eddy, the Discoverer and Founder of Christian Science, and her students, vastly increased the attendance at church services. So much so, that rented halls were no longer adequate for the church in Boston. A church home was mandatory.

The immediacy of the need at that time speaks to us from the pages of this book. Apathy, doubt, and fear intruded. Materiel procurement seemed impossible. Labor controversies caused innumerable delays. Shortages of funds plagued the members. Time schedules appeared incapable of fulfillment. And yet, so faithful was the prayerful reliance on divine Mind's control, the buildings—the Original Edifice, and later the Extension—were constructed on time, in complete conformity with architectural specifications.

As originally planned, the edifices were fully paid for prior to the dedicatory services. The record stands, an inspiration to every new branch church or Christian Science Society, telling how prayer can demonstrate the limitless resources of divine Mind.

The Church of Christ, Scientist, exists to spiritually enlighten, heal, and save. Its purpose is to eliminate spiritual

foreword

ignorance, heal sickness and disease, overcome sin and death. Designed to reflect the structure of divine reality, this Church proves the understanding of God to be practical in every phase of human experience.

This volume describes the erection of the Original Edifice of The Mother Church as told by Joseph Armstrong, and the building of the Extension as reported by Margaret Williamson. It records the inspired action of church members, under the leadership of Mrs. Eddy. The visible characteristics of these buildings were, as Miss Williamson writes of the Extension, "but the natural outward expression of an inward devotion, consecration, and development." [1]

This volume conveys eloquently the courage, perception, perseverance, and gratitude of those early workers. Their faith and fortitude, their love and expectancy, remain an inspiration for all who would build, and build again, in the name of Christian Science.

The account testifies persuasively to the advancing mission of the Church as described by Mary Baker Eddy: "From first to last The Mother Church seemed type and shadow of the warfare between the flesh and Spirit, even that shadow whose substance is the divine Spirit, imperatively propelling the greatest moral, physical, civil, and religious reform ever known on earth. In the words of the prophet: 'The shadow of a great rock in a weary land.' " [2]

It is healing that builds Churches of Christ, Scientist, and their edifices today. Nothing short of healing will do it. And the very construction of an edifice must be a healing in itself, the demonstration of divine Mind's government, direction, abundance, intelligence. Mindful of this, Christian Scientists will cherish the inspiration of this volume.

A brief Epilogue has been added, bringing the reader up to date on the completion of the Extension and the addition of the Sunday School and Church Administration buildings.

Arthur P. Wuth

[1] *The Mother Church Extension,* p. 2; [2] *Pulpit and Press,* p. 20.

The Original

preface

In this brief narrative of the erection of the original edifice of
The Mother Church, The First Church of Christ, Scientist, in
Boston, no attempt is made to elaborate the subject, or to
treat of matters that may be intimately connected with the
history of the church organization and may indirectly concern the structure, but do not bear directly on the details of
its erection.

The writer's aim is simply to state the facts as he knows
them, and little effort is made to point out the many beautiful lessons taught and illustrated by these experiences. It
seems desirable to preserve a record of at least a few of the
trials, toils, and triumphs of this laborious effort, not only for
the benefit of this age, but for the generations to come,
which may be able to see more fully than we now can the
meaning of this demonstration, and to realize that in the
building of this church a Christian endeavor was successful.

The Board of Directors, who for more than a year were
burdened with the heavy care and responsibility of erecting
the edifice, can never forget nor cease to thank God for the
wise guidance, the helpful words, and the loving care of our
teacher and mother, Mary Baker Eddy. She alone, God's chosen and anointed one, deserves the credit of this mighty victory for Mind's supremacy; for it was her warning call and
loving counsel that led on to success in the face of such
seeming odds. Her nearness to the great heart of Love

endowed her with power from on high before which every obstacle vanished.

The writer also wishes to thank our dear mother for the privilege of publishing in this book facsimiles of two of her beautiful letters to the Directors.

It is to be hoped the future will also give credit to those friends who, like obedient children, left all at the mother's call, and came to relieve the heavily burdened ones. We know our heavenly Father always will reward in due season.

To those whose donations have paid for this beautiful building, standing as a testimonial of love for her through whom the blessing of Christian Science has come, the writer would say: Be your contribution counted in thousands of dollars, or in single pennies, your reward is as sure as your existence.

Joseph Armstrong

the foundation

For other foundation can no man lay than that is laid, which is Jesus Christ. — I Corinthians 3:11

In September, 1893, Mary Baker Eddy, Discoverer and Founder of Christian Science, advised the Directors of The First Church of Christ, Scientist, in Boston, to lay the foundation for a church building the following October.

At this point the history of our present structure begins; but in order to describe accurately the condition of affairs at the time, it may be well to retrace briefly certain previous steps.

Our teacher had long been hoping for a church edifice in Boston, and for several years her students had been making efforts to fulfill her hope. In 1887-8 about four thousand dollars were contributed toward a building fund and a site was bought; but as the students could give only a small part of the price, the remainder was secured by a mortgage. This they were unable to pay when it became due, and the lot was sold by foreclosure to Mrs. Eddy. She immediately conveyed it to Ira O. Knapp, C.S.D., for the use of the church, a board of trustees being appointed to care for it.

About thirty thousand dollars was soon raised, enough to warrant those trustees in beginning the work; but they were unwilling to build unless the church, disorganized at Mrs. Eddy's request, was established under the laws of Massachusetts.

7

the foundation

Mrs. Eddy then took the lot again into her own name, and deeded it, in September, 1892, to four of her students, constituting them The Christian Science Board of Directors. This Board was to hold the land in trust for the whole body of Christian Scientists, a law having been discovered which permitted this to be done. The new deed required the Directors, Ira O. Knapp, William B. Johnson, Joseph S. Eastaman, and Stephen A. Chase, to erect a church edifice within five years at a cost of not less than fifty thousand dollars. In March, 1893, Captain Eastaman was succeeded by Joseph Armstrong, and it was upon the Board as thus constituted that the responsibility of erecting the building rested.

The money received by the first board of trustees was returned to the donors; and while this transfer was going on and the money was flowing back again into the treasury, the newly constituted Board of Directors was soliciting designs for the structure.

Several Boston architects drew plans for a brick building, one of these designs being more satisfactory than the others because it utilized the entire ground,—a result especially desired. On later consideration it seemed more appropriate to build the church of granite from New Hampshire, the native state and present home of the Discoverer and Founder of Christian Science; so the architects again made drawings, this time for a stone building. The architect who had excelled before once more presented the most acceptable plan, which not only covered the whole lot, but was the most beautiful in design. This lot being on a corner, and shaped somewhat like a kite, was thought to be awkwardly formed for a church site until this draft was seen, when it was at once acknowledged that the land could hardly be better adapted to our purpose.

This was the state of affairs when the Directors were advised to lay the foundation. Our teacher doubtless perceived the need of immediate action; for, although our fund now amounted to about forty thousand dollars, receipts had almost ceased, the students either thinking that enough had

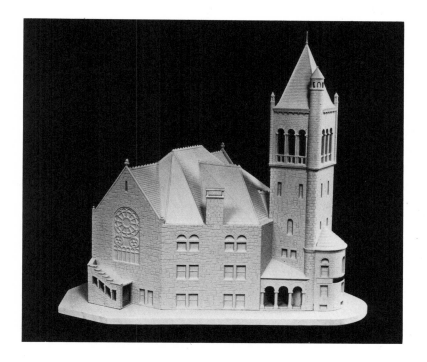

Architect's model

been already raised, or else fearing on account of the former experience that the money might be lost or otherwise fail of its purpose.

In obtaining estimates from builders, the Directors had already learned that, during the delay occasioned by hesitation over the land title, additional laws had been enacted, July 16, 1892, requiring such buildings to be fireproof; consequently, that to build a church now would cost a third more than before that date.

The Directors found themselves in a dilemma. On one side was the urgent need of beginning to build, while on the other hand they were confronted by lack of material means. If they decided to use brick, the new laws would increase the cost by many thousands of dollars more than had been as yet contributed, while stone would be even more expensive.

the foundation

According to city ordinances, plans must be municipally approved before a building permit could be issued; so the Directors must accept a design determining the cost of the completed building before they could obtain a permit or lay the foundation.

The deed of gift did not allow the property to be mortgaged. More money would doubtless be received while the work was going on; but who could say how much? With less than fifty thousand dollars on hand, how could the Directors incur so great a risk as to accept such expensive plans, in order to obtain a permit from the city? The advice from the teacher and mother to lay the foundation in October was, however, of greater importance than any other consideration; and those to whom the responsibility was entrusted finally decided to choose the most desirable plan and go forward,— leaving the result with God.

This decision was reached the last of September, and then the permit was anxiously desired so that work might be begun on the foundation; but much was yet to be done. The architect had furnished only the outlines of the roof, and it was found that a detailed plan of the iron or steel framework must be presented for the city engineer's inspection. To obtain the needful plan, estimates must be solicited for this part of the building. An estimate being accepted, the contractor would then make his own exact drawings.

The Directors were dissatisfied with the estimates submitted; but, in order to get the contractor's plan and the permit, they were compelled to make an immediate award of the roof contract. The lowest bid was accepted; but the contractor, for reasons unnecessary to relate, refused to keep his agreement or to submit specifications to the city. After delays of one kind and another, the official agreed to waive this point for future consideration; and late in October he granted the building permit.

In this experience regarding the roof may be recognized the hand of divine Love, guiding and protecting those who trust Him. Human law would have forced the Directors to

the foundation

obligate themselves for an expensive roof before any provision had been made for the foundation or for the walls on which the roof was to rest.

It may be well to mention here what was rather unusual, that the Directors, although still retaining the services of the architect, had become sole owners of his plans. It had been at first arranged that he should receive a percentage on the cost of building, one half payable on the bestowal of the contract, and the other when the church was completed. Before any contract was arranged, the architect desired an advance payment; and the result was that the Directors bought his plans outright, obtaining a bill of sale.

Such details, which may seem insignificant, had a greater influence on the erection of the church than may appear on the surface; and the writer, knowing their latent import, could not feel that his account would be complete if they were not noted.

The contracts for excavation, pile driving, and stone foundations were signed on October 19, 1893. The Charles River once overflowed much of the Back Bay region where the church lot is situated; and, so near the harbor, the water was affected by even the lowest tides. Foundation piles for building had to be driven down far enough to remain permanently under water, so as to be unaffected by atmospheric influences. It was at first thought that our piling must be driven eighteen or twenty feet below the foundation grade, but hard ground was struck much nearer the surface. A gentleman familiar with Back Bay before the land was filled in, states that our site was part of a point which was not always submerged. Be that as it may, solid bottom was found on which the piles could rest, thus insuring a firm foundation.

The first stone was laid Wednesday, November 8, 1893, and when the foundation wall was finished, it was carefully covered with boards for protection during the winter.

This demonstration, an actual beginning, inspired Christian Science workers in the field with such confidence and energy that money once more began to flow into the treasurer's hands.

the great contract

The God of heaven, he will prosper us; therefore we his servants will arise and build. — Nehemiah 2:20

I will direct their work in truth, and I will make an everlasting covenant with them. — Isaiah 61:8

As soon as arrangements had been completed for the foundation, Mrs. Eddy recommended that preparations be made for beginning work on the church itself early in the ensuing spring, and that the work be finished in the same year, 1894.

Money was coming in all the time, and there might be thirty thousand dollars left after the payments were made for the foundation; but what was this with which to contract for such a building as was desired? The Directors, however, were beginning to learn that "with God all things are possible" [1] though His ways are not man's ways. They knew that God was speaking through their teacher, and would guide them in the right direction, if they would follow willingly and obediently. With scarcely one third of the needful money on hand, and debt forbidden, it seemed unreasonable to think of contracting for so costly a building; but the voice of Truth was imperative, and something must be done.

After careful and prayerful consideration of the problem many days and nights, the Directors decided that they might begin and build at least the walls.

Several of the best-known builders in the city were asked

[1] Matt. 19:26.

for estimates; but many of them refused, making it difficult for the Directors to select the most reliable parties for so important an undertaking. Responsible New Hampshire builders were found, however, who offered to erect the brick and stone walls, with the necessary iron or steel beams, for a reasonable amount; yet the price was much greater than the present fund. To promise a dollar beyond the assets would be a forfeiture of the land title; and the Directors had already made it a rule to base no calculations on pledges or promises of money, but to act only on what was in their possession.

Mrs. Eddy had not been informed of the situation, nor of the mental struggle it was causing the Directors, yet a letter from her solved the whole problem. She suggested that a contract might be made for the walls, which would include a provision giving the Directors a right to stop the work at any time after the masonry had risen above the level of the auditorium floor; that is, of course, if parties could be found who would enter into such an unusual arrangement. It seemed wise to have but one contract for this part of the work.

The New Hampshire men were found perfectly willing to enter into the conditional agreement, and the papers were signed, December 6, 1893, by the four Directors on one side and on the other side by three men representing as many firms, which were not only to build the walls, but to furnish brick, iron, and the gray and pink granite. Thus it reads:

> The party of the second part [the Directors] to have the privilege to stop the work, at any point above the level of the audience-room floor, on four weeks' notice; and the work to be resumed on four weeks' notice, provided that not over one year shall intervene between the time of stopping and starting the same; and, if not stopped by the party of the second part, said contract shall be finished on or before August first, 1894.

The document further stipulated that the contractors had until September to finish the tower, from a point ten feet above the walls of the main building. Eighty per cent of the work actually completed was to be paid for at the end of each month; and the remaining twenty per cent when the work was finally completed "to the satisfaction of the Directors." This last clause was somewhat out of the ordinary form, which requires the approval of the architect alone.

Before a single layer was begun on the walls, our teacher and mother, consulting only with infinite Mind, quietly wrote to certain students, offering them the privilege of contributing a thousand dollars each to the building fund. In response to this offer, forty-four thousand dollars were added to our supply, which, together with what had been coming in as usual, assured the contractors that they could go on with the work to completion.

the iron question and the cornerstone

Except the Lord build the house, they labour in vain that build it. — Psalm
127:1
Upon this rock I will build my church; and the gates of hell shall not pre-
vail against it. — Matthew 16:18

March began with excellent weather for wall building; but, to
the Directors' surprise, the work was not begun. A visit of inquiry to Concord and Woodsville, New Hampshire, where
the contractors resided, brought an assurance that all was
right, and labor would begin at once. April came, however,
and nothing had been accomplished; not even the necessary
municipal permit had been obtained for the use of the street
during the process of building.

The contractors were then summoned to Boston, and the
reason for the delay was discovered to be a deadlock between the builders and the firm from which they expected to
buy the iron or steel beams. The Directors had been informed that the metal was bought in December, and they
never dreamed of trouble in this direction. Now it appeared
that the proposed purchase had never been completed because of a difference of opinion between architect and dealer
as to the amount of iron called for by the plans. On the
insistence of the Directors, an agreement was reached, and

the iron question and the cornerstone

part of the iron was promised in ten days, the rest to follow at intervals sufficient to prevent further delay in building.

Mrs. Eddy had already been asking when the Directors would be ready to lay the cornerstone; but they were unable to answer the question, for as yet only a small quantity of stone had been delivered.

One of the contractors remained in Boston to commence operations, and the next point to be gained was to obtain a permit from the city for the use of the street while building. The fact that he did not live in the state made the matter somewhat troublesome, for he must give bond to provide for any possible cases of accident, and must have a resident bondsman. This was adjusted satisfactorily, the permit at last gained, the exact lines of the building lot located by a surveyor, and the first stone of the church wall laid April 24.

The first supply of iron from Pennsylvania did not arrive when promised, and at nearly the same time the Directors were advised to fix upon May 1 as the date for laying the cornerstone.

According to the design, this stone was to rest in the wall over an arch which must first be spanned by four heavy curved iron beams. How were these beams to be obtained in time? Two plans were proposed: one, that a Director go to Pennsylvania, see that this indispensable iron was at once shipped, and follow it to its destination; the other, that the curved beams be bought in Boston, at the Directors' personal expense. Both suggestions were rejected on the grounds that a journey to Pennsylvania would interfere with the contracting manufacturers and to buy the iron at home would be to pay for it twice. Our teacher and mother was consulted, and the date for laying the cornerstone was postponed.

The pressure to go forward and do something became more imperative every day, while at the same time everything material claimed to discourage and hinder the Directors, "fears within and foes without." The stronger the demand the more impossible it seemed to obtain materials or to advance the work.

the iron question and the cornerstone

All this time, during the month of May, almost nothing could be done because no iron had arrived. Upon the foundation was to be built a twenty-inch brick wall faced with eight inches of gray granite. All that had been done up to this time, all that could be done until the beams were in place, was to lay the stone face and a part of its brick backing, leaving projecting bricks and iron bars with which to tie the whole together when the rest of the brick could be laid.

Several feet of this incomplete wall had been built when further counsel from our teacher and mother designated May 21, 1894, as the day for laying the cornerstone.

To make sure that it was on hand when needed, the Directors had already sent for this stone, and it was now in the little wooden shanty put up as an office for the use of the contractors near the corner itself. The stone was to have been polished and engraved at the quarry but, not being quite ready when sent for, was finished on the church grounds. The copper receptacle for memorial books and papers had also been provided, so that everything was ready except the wall where the stone must be laid.

To get the curved iron beams from Pennsylvania in accordance with the contract, for May 21, proved to be impossible, and it seemed unwise to postpone the date again; so the beams were ordered from a Boston firm which promised, as the best they could do, that the iron should be delivered by May 20.

Three days before the stone was to be placed, the Directors met at the Christian Science publishing house, then on Boylston Street, where the copper box was in readiness, and the following articles, wrapped separately in oiled silk, were put within it:

THE BIBLE, *in finest morocco binding.*

SCIENCE AND HEALTH WITH KEY TO THE SCRIPTURES, by Mary Baker G. Eddy, *eighty-fourth edition, in the same size and binding as the copy of the Bible.*

17

the iron question and the cornerstone

Also, by the same author:

RETROSPECTION AND INTROSPECTION.

UNITY OF GOOD.

NO AND YES.

RUDIMENTAL DIVINE SCIENCE.

THE PEOPLE'S IDEA OF GOD.

CHRISTIAN HEALING.

HISTORICAL SKETCH OF CHRISTIAN SCIENCE MIND-HEALING.

DEFENCE OF CHRISTIAN SCIENCE (out of print, a copy being furnished by a student).

Five Numbers of the CHRISTIAN SCIENCE SERIES.

AN ADDRESS, in manuscript, written for the occasion.

Besides these:

THE CHRISTIAN SCIENCE JOURNAL, June, 1894.

THE CHRISTIAN SCIENCE QUARTERLY BIBLE LESSONS, for April, May, and June, 1894.

THREE CARDS: the first containing a list of the students who contributed one thousand dollars each to the building fund; the second, a grateful acknowledgment of the same by our teacher; the third, a list of the Board of Directors, written by Mrs. Eddy's own hand.

The Directors took the box to the factory which had furnished it, where they saw it hermetically sealed, and then drove with it to the church site. It was about half-past five in the afternoon. The workmen were just leaving, and the carriage waited down the street till all but the superintendent had gone. Alone, the Directors entered the little shanty where the stone lay, and put the sealed box in its resting place. A copy of the mother's address was read (the original being already in the box), the iron lid was fitted into the stone over the coffer, and the superintendent was called in to cement it firmly into place.

It had already been decided by the Directors that the stone with its valuable contents should not be out of their sight or that of some trusty individual until permanently placed in the wall. Accordingly, two young men, James A. Neal and Thomas W. Hatten, students of Mrs. Eddy's, had been

the iron question and the cornerstone

chosen as watchers; and they remained in the shanty three stormy nights, while one of the Directors stayed there during the daytime. So was this precious stone guarded every moment.

These busy days went by, but still no iron came from Pennsylvania. Students were blaming those in charge for all delays, but suggested no remedy for the difficulties, while our contractors seemed utterly helpless. The Directors saw they must take the iron question into their own hands; and accordingly, on May 19, they sent one of their number to Pennsylvania to remain until the iron, at least for the first floor, was shipped, and then to trace its course to Boston.

On his arrival, this Director found that nothing had been done at the mill; but when he explained to the proprietors what was wanted, they agreed to put all their forces on this job day and night and finish it at the earliest possible moment.

Monday morning, May 21, three of the Directors, the fourth being in Pennsylvania, met on the grounds. They found that the superintendent of the building had been called away for the day, a most unusual and unexpected thing, leaving in charge only a foreman who had but little idea of the plan of the work. It was declared impossible that the wall could be made ready that day.

The Directors were obliged to take charge of affairs themselves; and calling every man on the grounds to one point, they had the work begun of preparing the place for the cornerstone. The long curved iron beams were slowly laid over the piers,—a difficult process because of the weight and shape of the beams,—and at last bolted securely together. Then the wall was begun, and was almost finished when it was discovered that the stones fitted and shaped for the rounded corner were laid too far to one side for the ground plan; so it was necessary to take down the masonry and begin again.

Finally all was ready. The cornerstone was put on rollers

The cornerstone in place

and pushed into place by hand. Then the workmen withdrew. The three Directors uncovered their heads and, laying each a hand on the stone, they prayed silently and repeated the Lord's Prayer in unison.

So the simple ceremony was performed at close of day, alone with God; and, as the mother had quoted in a letter on this subject, "His voice was not heard in the street." The sun, which had been behind the clouds for three days, burst forth in brightness just at this moment and shone upon the cornerstone.

contracts and contractors

And they gave the money, being told, into the hands of them that did the work, . . . to the carpenters and builders, that wrought upon the house of the Lord. — II Kings 12:11
We are troubled on every side, yet not distressed; we are perplexed, but not in despair. — II Corinthians 4:8

Soon after the laying of the cornerstone, the absent Director returned from Pennsylvania, with a portion of the ironwork for the first floor. He had been absent two weeks. After watching the manufacturing process day and night he had followed the iron from point to point on its journey, tracing its entire course to the last change, and had thus prevented the freight car from being sidetracked or otherwise hindered. The arrival of this iron proved that each single demonstration, each effort to be obedient, makes the next step possible.

Larger foundation stones had been used than the contract required, and this necessitated the floor beams being made correspondingly shorter. The alteration was noticed in time for the architect to make a new drawing, which he forwarded to the Boston iron contractor; he in turn sent the sketch to the Pennsylvania mill, but without instructions as to what it signified. He then informed the architect that, as the beams were already rolled, their recutting would cost twenty-five dollars. The statement was incorrect, for the ironwork had not yet been touched.

A month later, when the work was really done, no attention was paid to the altered measurements on the architect's last drawing; consequently, when the beams arrived they were found to be too long. This caused delay, but the difficulty was overcome by chipping off the stone so as to allow the beams more space in the wall.

Meantime the Directors were being troubled by another problem. The building fund was still insufficient to guarantee all the contracts required for different parts of the church, but it was now time that plans should be settled and agreements made for the entire work. From this time to the end these questions were constantly to be considered: what section must next be built in order to protect and strengthen what is already done? what work must be put in at the same time other parts are being constructed? what contracts will require most time for obtaining necessary materials? Most urgent of all was this question: what can be paid for?

There should be a contract for the roof in order that the iron frame be made in time and the roofer have his materials ready for finishing as soon as the walls were up. As fast, therefore, as the necessary amount was in the hands of the treasurer contracts were signed to meet the more pressing demands, the Directors now making each individual agreement themselves so as to bring matters more under their immediate care and avoid all possible mistakes or delays.

Near the end of June it became evident that the iron columns for the support of the auditorium and galleries would be needed very soon, and the builders were so notified. This iron, like the floor beams, was part of the original "great contract" and had been sublet to some Massachusetts manufacturers. After much urging, several columns were delivered, but upon examination they proved to be altogether unfit for use. The company insisted that they were good and refused to replace them. The first week in July the columns were furnished, but the city inspector of buildings, who examined every part of the work as it progressed, condemned the entire lot. Nevertheless, the firm still claimed that their castings should be accepted.

contracts and contractors

It was the middle of July. There was no prospect of continuing the work under two weeks; if the order were to be duplicated from the same mill, the delay might be indefinite. Another firm was found which agreed to furnish this iron to our contractors in two weeks. Even then, when the columns were delivered, several days more must be spent in setting them up and laying the beams upon them so that the work on the walls, which had come to a standstill, could be resumed. This at the best meant nearly a month of lost time.

During the delay practically nothing was done. All the workmen left except two or three stonelayers and one bricklayer. The iron foundry was prompt, however; and before the specified time enough columns were ready so that the work could begin again.

The building advanced rapidly for a time but it was not long before progress was again impeded. The floor beams were slow in coming, and many were not drilled in the proper places. To rectify all this was slow work, and the weary days dragged on through August and September. Once more the same Director was sent to Pennsylvania, where he remained till he saw all the iron of the contract manufactured and shipped. There was, therefore, no more hindrance from this quarter except for the cutting and fitting of the beams.

The discontent of the masons was causing great inconvenience. It was customary for masons to be paid weekly, but the contractors sometimes neglected to provide the money as often as once in two weeks. When the men threatened to quit work, the builders would have let them go but in order to prevent delays the Directors advanced the amount. On one occasion the money to pay the men was collected from the Christian Science students who happened to be on the premises. After this the Directors reserved a sufficient sum from their monthly settlement with the contractors to ensure the wages of the laborers.

The iron frame was to have been placed on the roof between August 20 and September 10 but at this period the walls were very far from completion, nor was the roofer ready with his iron. A railroad strike in Chicago had cut off from the mills their supply of coal so that the metal could not be molded when promised.

Not until the last of September did the roof iron begin to arrive. It was hoped the frame would be set up in a few days but in this as in so many other things there was disappointment. The contractor found many excuses for postponement and when he finally announced himself ready to begin, two weeks were spent in erecting scaffolds and derricks. At last, after all these tedious delays which seemed so unnecessary to the Directors, the roof work was fairly under way and the contractor was urged to add to his force until he had as many men on the building as could be profitably employed.

At every step difficulties multiplied and affairs became more and more complicated till the completion of the church within the time specified seemed impossible. The struggle grew harder and more hopeless, to human sense, as each day brought its added burden as if one must make a journey upon which life depended, yet could find no train; when that was found or built, no engine; then, no coal, no track, and so on, with impediments multiplying at each step almost beyond imagination. Nevertheless, the Directors knew that God was directing our teacher and mother and that He would not demand the unachievable of so faithful a servant. This knowledge and faith gave them strength to press on; even as the children of Israel looked to Moses to lead them safely through the wilderness, so they had confidence that God would, through their Leader, show the way out of this apparently desperate condition.

It was clear that if the church was to be completed in 1894 the final contracts for the interior should be made at once; yet no liability could be incurred beyond the limits of the money on hand which was not yet sufficient to finish the structure. Those who knew nothing of these conditions insisted that all contracts be closed at once but the Directors, striving to be faithful to their trust and to their own highest sense of right, continued to follow the wise guidance of God's chosen one.

All this time the author had hoped for some way of escape from what seemed such an impossibility as to complete the church within the appointed year, but after a visit to the mother and a brief conversation with her about the building his doubts vanished forever. Like Elisha's servant when his eyes were opened, he saw that "they that be with us are more than they that be with them," [1] and from this hour he knew as an absolute certainty that, whatever the seeming, *the work would be done!*

On October 18 our teacher requested one of the Directors to take especial charge of the work and give it all his time.

For a month past three workmen had been engraving an inscription on the pink granite tablet built into the circular tower wall. On October 20 the work was completed, and the boards of the staging were knocked off so the words could be seen. The first sight of this inscription was most impressive even to those who knew how it was to read:

THE FIRST CHURCH OF CHRIST, SCIENTIST.
Erected Anno Domini, 1894.
A Testimonial to our beloved Teacher, the Reverend Mary Baker Eddy;
Discoverer and Founder of Christian Science; Author of its text-book,
SCIENCE AND HEALTH with KEY TO THE SCRIPTURES; President of the
Massachusetts Metaphysical College, and the first Pastor of this Denomination

During this month a contract for stained glass was concluded with the firm that seemed best able to bring out the ideas of Christian Science in this direction. One of the contractors had spent some time in Europe visiting the great churches. He showed much interest in developing designs for interior decoration and was employed by the Directors to procure samples of material from the different dealers in order to determine a color scheme that would harmonize with the glass. There were brought together samples of carpets and material for cushions, marble for dado, baseboard and

[1] See II Kings 6:14-17.

25

Testimonial inscription on the tower wall is completed

stairs, besides specimens of the wood which had already been ordered for the pews, and fresco designs for which estimates had been submitted. At a meeting held to decide these details the tints for all materials were chosen.

Less easy was a decision about the flooring, and for some time it seemed impossible to decide what should be used. Mosaic was desired for floors as well as dados; but this was not only more costly than wood, but required more time,— now an important consideration. At the last possible moment enough money came in to warrant a choice of the preferred material. The contractor would not promise his work in less than two months, even including extra night hours, and even after the Directors had agreed to his estimates there was a suspense of several days while he was considering whether, after all, he would undertake the job.

As the time grew shorter more and more questions pressed for settlement, each seeming more difficult than the last. Funds were still insufficient, and great care was needed for the wise expenditure of such contributions as the treasurer held at the moment.

The interior of the building showed nothing but rough brick walls, bare iron floor beams and dreary piles of *débris;* while mechanics and builders were declaring that it would require six months' more work to make the place ready for use.

Under this pressure the Directors struggled on through October and came to November, while everything seemed to be saying: "You cannot finish the church in 1894!"

All these months there was beautiful weather with scarcely any rain,—a remarkable season. On the morning of November 6 the church, unprotected by roof, floor or window, was full of snow,—the earliest that had fallen in the city for many years. From this time on, though the work never ceased, the weather was frequently something to contend against.

Yet, confronted by this fearful array of material evidence, the Directors pushed on with unfaltering trust in the divine omnipresent power of God.

help and shelter

He that dwelleth in the secret place of the most High shall abide under the shadow of the Almighty. I will say of the Lord, He is my refuge and my fortress: my God; in him will I trust. — Psalm 91:1, 2

The contract for heating and ventilating apparatus was given to Edward P. Bates, C.S.D., of Syracuse, New York, who, after arranging his own business, placed his whole time at the service of the Directors. The offer was accepted, and from November 12 till the building was entirely finished, he, with Mrs. Bates, remained in Boston constantly. As Mr. Bates had had much experience in building and his wife also was familiar with the technicalities of architectural plans, they proved invaluable assistants, bringing into the work fresh ideas as well as new courage.

As one result, another architect, with his draughtsman, was employed to assist in improving the interior designs, the former leaving his office in Hartford, Connecticut, in order to give his entire attention to our church.

Besides one woman who was already giving her time to the work, Mrs. Caroline W. Frame, C.S.B., of New York City, and Mrs. Emilie B. Hulin, C.S.B., of Brooklyn, New York, were called to Boston to assist in our progress. They devoted themselves to selecting furniture and fittings for "Mother's Room." All questions must be deferred to the Directors for final decision, yet their taste and experience in house furnishing was of great value. They also looked after the windows, to urge the work forward, see that the subjects were properly brought out, and that all was made harmonious.

The original plan had been to finish the auditorium and "Mother's Room" in wood; but now marble was suggested, and the arched entrance to "Mother's Room" was designed. It was also decided to raise the ceiling of the auditorium three feet and omit the plastered beams and panels as first designed.

The contract for roofing included terra cotta, ready roofing of paper, slate, and copper guttering; the terra cotta work had been let to the same firm which was to attend to the fire-proofing of the floors. The foreman for all this business was a man of great executive ability who took much interest in the building.

As soon as the iron roof frame was in place the roofer was daily urged to employ more help, in order to hasten this most needed part of the building. He began with only two or three men, and even after a week's continued urging only a few more had been employed. The foreman then explained that he had engaged thirty different men during this time but as soon as they were required to go on the roof they seemed stricken with fear. Some would go up only to come down immediately and slip away without a word; others would not even mount but only look up at the roof and then walk off. When the Directors learned this fact the difficulty was overcome, and in two days all the men needed were at work.

While the terra cotta did not wholly exclude rain, still it made quite a shelter; and it was therefore a surprise to find that the roofers, after laying the blocks from the summit down to within five feet of the gutter, ceased work, leaving this space uncovered all around the building. On inquiry it appeared that the architect had been persuaded by the roof contractor to change the plans for the gutters. This change would require extending the entire iron frame five feet and would mean several weeks' delay. Therefore, the new arrangement was countermanded at once, and the contractor was ordered to begin again on the original plan which he

Construction proceeds

himself had approved when the contract was originally entered into.

Once more work was resumed but again ceased. The contractor claimed that if the blocks were laid to the outer edge of the roof the water would thereby be conducted into the walls where it would freeze and throw them down. The Directors were unwilling to accept this excuse and two of them went at once to the office of the roofing company to see about having the work finished according to agreement.

The company was one of the oldest and most reliable in Boston. During the conversation with the members present every argument and excuse they could bring forward,—in regard to weather, for example,—was so answered that at last the senior partner had to admit that the work could continue without interruption and even promised to be at the church himself the next morning to see that operations were resumed. There were still many difficulties to overcome before the roof was finished but nothing else caused so much delay.

The Director in charge, with his assistants, now found it necessary to oversee the work continually, and remained on the premises all day and a part of the night. By the middle of November the roof was closed in with terra cotta, and window openings were covered with canvas. The interior was heated by stoves and lighted with electricity so that work might continue until midnight or even later, if need be.

It was in the evening that most of the fireproofing was laid in the floors and concreted over,—first in the auditorium and then in the vestry. The only risk in laying these floors before the roof was complete was that water might drip through upon them and freeze, but this never occurred. These hollow terra cotta bricks, about ten inches long by six in width and thickness, are not only fireproof, but are very light and strong. The blocks are cemented together between the iron beams of the floor frame resting on its flanged edges, and in twenty-four hours, when the cement has set, are solid and capable of resisting great pressure.

One morning, when after a long struggle plenty of men

were at last on hand for the work on the floors, one of the masons looked up and exclaimed: "Well, sir, I believe you'll get it done!" He meant that the church would be ready for use at the appointed time. This was in a dark hour, when even those from whom testimony opposed to the senses was expected, lacked faith to voice an assurance such as this. Many students, visiting the place, would look blankly at the bare walls and say: "You can't get it done, can you?"

Like a message from heaven came the following lines, quoted by our teacher and mother to lighten these heavy days and increase our confidence in her perpetual elevation above the clouds of sense:

Friday, 10 a.m., November 23, 1894.

TO THE C. S. BOARD OF DIRECTORS

When the mists have risen above us,
As our Father knows His own,
Face to face with those who love us,
We shall know as we are known.
Love, beyond the Orient meadows,
Floats the golden fringe of day;
Heart to heart we bide the shadows,
Till the mists have cleared away.

MOTHER.

a night's work

In the daytime also he led them with a cloud, and all the night with a light
of fire. — Psalm 78:14
So the workmen wrought, and the work was perfected by them, and they
set the house of God in his state. — II Chronicles 24:13

The ready roofing being laid over the terra cotta and the gutters cemented with pitch, the roof was practically watertight
and could thus stand for months. While the slate and copper
were being put on there were several heavy rains and some
snow; yet this caused no uneasiness as the work on the interior could continue without hindrance. Neither was the finishing of the exterior delayed by the weather, for, through all
the wind and storm of November and December the work
advanced steadily, although sometimes the roofers were
obliged to shovel off the snow before beginning their daily
work.

As soon as the roof would keep out water and the walls
were in a proper condition it was expected that the plasterer
would set his men to work without waiting for other parts of
the church to be finished; but this was not in accord with his
ideas for he expected to have the building exclusively to himself for some eight weeks. Valuable time was lost over this
point, and but little accomplished.

Meantime the iron frame for the vaulted ceiling was getting into place. As fast as one part was prepared it was desirable that the wire lathing should at once be added in order to

make ready for plastering. The contractor being still reluctant to work in what seemed to him so irregular a fashion, here was more delay; but at length he agreed to let his men work one night, with extra wages assured and the Directors furnishing light and heat. The arrangement was that as many men as feasible should be set to work on the auditorium ceiling which would be the longest job, the strips under the galleries having already been plastered at intervals when other mechanics were not in the way.

The night selected was Saturday, December 8, with the hope that the work would be finished before morning and the plaster dry during the Sunday following. Scaffolding had been put up a day or two before; so, when the plaster was provided, there was nothing more to do but mix it with water and apply it to walls and ceiling. A patent preparation which dries very quickly was to be used. It is powdered like flour and can be brought into a building in bags and piled up ready for use.

On Saturday morning the contractor agreed to have enough material on hand to begin work by five in the afternoon, but about three o'clock, when at least seventeen tons of dry plaster were expected, one lone team drove up through the dismal rain and fog and stopped at the church. Upon inquiry it was learned that no arrangement had been made for delivering more than this one load of four tons.

Something must be done at once or all this labor and planning to save a few hours' time would be lost. The Directors tried immediately by telephone to find out if this driver could not be allowed to bring another load, but after half an hour's waiting for a clear line word came that the team could not be out any longer.

Effort was then made to communicate with the plaster warehouse and, after more delay, the agent was reached just as he was locking up for the night. "You must be insane!" was his first reply over the telephone to a request that sixteen tons more of plaster be sent at once. After some explanatory debate, he went out to look for teams and shortly returned to the wire with the welcome message that three teams more were already loaded and a fourth team would be soon on the road. By nine o'clock all the bags were lying on the church floor.

Unless the plasterers could work the full hours agreed upon they refused to do anything, but before time for the long labor to begin it was known that more material was coming, and at five o'clock there were fifteen men mixing the plaster and some fifteen more ready to put it on. All seemed inspired with energy and activity, and spectators long acquainted with such work declared they had never seen plasterers cover space so rapidly and so well. The workmen themselves were amazed at what was accomplished. The Scientists in charge remained to encourage and cheer every effort, and by morning two coats of plaster were on the auditorium. Thus was a great victory won.

Monday, December 10, the finishing touches were put on the ceiling, and Thursday of the same week the painters began to do their part.

the harmony of trades

Speaking the truth in love, may [we] grow up into him in all things, which is the head, even Christ: from whom the whole body fitly joined together and compacted by that which every joint supplieth, according to the effectual working in the measure of every part, maketh increase of the body unto the edifying of itself in love. — Ephesians 4:15, 16

From the middle of September to December 1, the great problem to be solved had been, How can it be managed so that mechanics of different trades shall work together simultaneously on the church? This must be done if the building was to be finished in 1894; yet each contractor in turn expected and demanded to have the place cleared of all workmen except his own. When the Directors asked any one contractor to go to work while others were still busy, each declared it impossible. In every case this caused a delay of two or three days. Then each contractor would agree to make the trial, while the Directors on their part promised to see that no other contractor interfered.

The staging for the iron roof frame was erected, and work begun on the roof, before the walls were finished. Next the plumbers, who like all the other contractors were behind with their work, began operations. As soon as the roof frame was in place, men began putting on the terra cotta blocks and other roofing materials at the same time the terra cotta slabs and concrete were being laid for the floors. When a part of the floor blocks were laid and concreted over the mosaic work was commenced, and while these various undertakings were getting under way the iron frame for the ceiling was being put up, and still other contractors were finding places for their men.

The mosaic was laid around the bottoms of the heavy posts that upheld the staging for the ceiling work. As fast as a part of the iron was in place this staging was removed and the spaces where the posts had stood were filled in with mosaic.

Bits of mud and iron, and occasionally a tool, would fall from the hands above, but nobody below was in the least injured.

The only accident that occurred during the building was to a painter, who stepped through a hole in the unfinished vestry floor and sprained his ankle. A Christian Scientist came at once to his aid and relieved him of pain. His contracting employer, however, fearing there might be damages to pay, insisted that the man be sent to the railroad station in a cab and return to his home in the suburbs where he resided about ten minutes' walk from the station. The next morning he was able to run to catch his train in order promptly to resume his place.

As the work progressed with wonderful rapidity, other mechanics began their labor, side by side with those already busy, until, by December 1, every industry having aught to do with building the church was represented there, making a force of some two hundred men. To keep them moving together harmoniously meant rapid and continuous action by those in charge. No one set of laborers must be allowed to fall behind lest this disturb some other set and bring the work to a standstill, for the men could labor together only in proportion as the work of each separate trade was kept out of the way of that following.

The Director in charge who had full authority to decide any question must every few minutes visit all parts of the work as it advanced because the different gangs of men all protested at working in company and were held together only by the Directors' promise that one trade should not interfere with or trespass on the rights of another.

Questions were continually arising as to how this or that should be done. One change would often necessitate another, and in connection with the question of how something should be done was always the underlying question of expense.

It is certainly worthy of note, as showing that the power of Mind was really building our church, that these solutions of mechanical difficulties—often accomplished by one without experience in this particular branch of labor and with no architectural plan at hand for consultation—were always accepted by the workmen, and proved satisfactory.

Although, as has just been said, the matter of cost had always to be considered,—and this necessity continued until the award of the very last contract,—yet it should be stated that the question of money scarcely affected the building of the church. Beginning with October, the treasurer was advised to tell no one what funds were on hand. Even the Directors could only ask him, Can such or such a thing be afforded? But, as often happened, while the Directors were deciding which material or design to choose, enough money would be received during the time of deliberation to render the price no longer a prime consideration and leave them free to adopt the most appropriate, though sometimes the most expensive, suggestion. The last month's contributions were very generous but the Directors were careful of expense until the very end.

The municipal permit for using the streets bounding the church lot included only the Falmouth Street side. The way on the north side, now called Norway Street, had not then been accepted by the city but it was lawful for the contractors to use one half the width of this street for unloading, mixing cement, and preparing other materials. At a time when loads were arriving hourly and every foot of space was needed, Norway Street was accepted by the city, a contract was made for a sewer pipe to be laid, and the builders were ordered to move their effects immediately. Much of the work had therefore to be abandoned for a few days till arrangements could be made for workmen and materials in the narrow limits of Falmouth Street.

The laborers who had been busy on this side thought themselves already overcrowded, and when called upon to share their space with the workmen from Norway Street they set up a strong protest; but the Director in charge, knowing that in divine Mind no man can encroach upon his neighbor, assured the men they need fear no interference or molestation. Soon all found places, and the work went on as smoothly as if each mechanic had the street to himself. The Director thanked God for deliverance and took courage.

To give some idea of what was done during the month of December besides the superintendence of the work, the following list of contracts is given, with the dates when they were signed:

Decorations, December 5.
Vestry chairs, December 5.
Marble, December 6.
Pulpit, and the furniture for "Mother's Room," December 7.
Electric fixtures, December 8.
Marble for "Mother's Room," December 12.
Stereo-relief work, December 13.
Sidewalk, December 14.
Bronze torches and brackets, December 18.
Onyx mantel for "Mother's Room," December 20.

From the first of December to the morning of January 6 no busier place than our church could have been found in Boston. The whole structure, within and without, was alive with workmen. Heavily loaded teams were arriving at all hours during the day and far into the night and the creak of wheels and derricks was constantly heard as roofing materials, brick and stone were being raised by hand or steam to roof and tower. Plaster, paint, glass and other materials for interior finish, were being carried up the long planks through the church door, and to all these indications of activity were added the calls from workmen above, giving orders and directions, answered by those beneath.

Inside the building from boiler room to auditorium ceiling a still more active scene met the eye, if that were possible. Concrete was being mixed and spread in one part, mosaic laid in another; the painter followed close after the plasterer; the plumber, the electrician and workmen putting in the heating and ventilating apparatus mingled with the others; a constant stream of laborers clattered up and down the unfinished stairs, carrying in new material or taking out rubbish.

Every workman seemed to feel the importance of punctually finishing the work. Among the different contractors and their gangs of employees there was never a word of dispute. On the contrary, it was remarkable how carefully each artisan recognized the rights of every other. Side by side with artists setting delicate pieces of colored glass were those chiseling and hammering the metal casements or the iron staircases. The beautiful onyx mantel was put up in the "Mother's Room" at the same time that rougher work was being done, yet nothing was injured and no man interfered with his neighbor.

About the middle of December, the auditorium was filled with the scaffolding for the plasterers, and on every stage of it men were busy plastering, painting, decorating and fitting in the sunburst and windows. The mosaic floor had been laid but was covered with heavy paper and boards to prevent soiling from paint and plaster. The dado was being set, with marble baseboard and cap. Gallery posts were being wire-lathed and plastered. The stereo-relief contractor had just begun his work. Electric fixtures were being put in, doors fitted and hung, and terra cotta laid in the gallery. Everybody seemed in earnest, anxious to accomplish as much as possible. The buzzing of the sawing machine, cutting metal for window frames, the clank of steel tools upon the stairs, the pounding of wooden hammers on mosaic floors,—these were the sounds that rose above the general hum of activity.

Surely it can be said that no other building was ever

erected in such a way. When Solomon built his temple the men who wrought were personally interested therein and worldly wealth was at their service, but in our church all things material seemed opposed to its advancement.

In this harmonious working of the trades, and the earnest effort to finish on time was recognized the hand of our heavenly Father, turning back the armies of the aliens, bringing to naught the plans of the wicked, and revealing Himself as divine Principle, governing human affairs. It was a new demonstration of the oneness of divine Mind and the universal brotherhood of man; of the nothingness of material, and the omnipotence of spiritual law, as taught in Christian Science.

testimonial windows and other gifts

And I will make thy windows of agates, and thy gates of carbuncles, and
all thy borders of pleasant stones. — Isaiah 54:12
Let us be glad and rejoice, and give honour to him: for the marriage of the
Lamb is come, and his wife hath made herself ready. — Revelation 19:7

Soon after the work on the building was fairly started, different churches and societies in our ranks, as well as individual
students, began to ask for the privilege of paying for special
objects. This was granted, on condition that the money be
turned over to the treasurer of the building fund and the gifts
be subject to whatever changes our teacher and mother or
the Directors might think necessary.

In this way were purchased doors, dado for stairways and
vestibules, electric fixtures, mosaic floors, marble window
sills and treads for the vestibule steps, cushions and platform, the pulpit and its furnishings, with handsome copies of
the Bible and *Science and Health with Key to the Scriptures*, the
mother's chair, to be kept on the rostrum, contribution bas-
kets with extension handles invented by the giver, and the
tubular chime of fifteen bells. The concert grand Steinway
piano for the vestry was the donation of one young lady, but
the chief single benefaction, costing several thousand dollars,
was the organ,—one of the finest in Boston,—a tribute of

gratitude from a gentleman whose wife had been healed through Christian Science.

In the middle of November a student came from the West to see about furnishing the church with bronze doors, but the expense was so much more than he expected that after a week's investigation the project was abandoned and the money given for a window and the general fund.

A well lighted auditorium had been especially desired by the Directors as one of the chief characteristics of the church, but as it became evident that the painted figures and colored glass would admit only a dim and subdued light, some further means of letting in the sunshine must be adopted. Someone suggested that light be let in from above, but this seemed impracticable. The architect was consulted, as well as others who might have ideas on the subject, and as the roof had not yet been constructed, the plans were examined to ascertain where an opening could be made. It was found feasible, with slight additional expense, to insert a skylight, measuring ten feet by twenty, directly above the auditorium ceiling.

What could be used in the ceiling itself to let through the light thus secured from the roof above? This was the next question, for such an adjunct must not only be ornamental in itself but harmonize with the decorations of the interior. After many plans had been examined and many suggestions received from artists and students, the beautiful sunburst now in use was selected, with its one hundred and forty-four electric lamps for additional illumination.

To insure still more light and forestall any possible darkening of the windows by the erection of high walls on adjacent lots, the architect planned three light shafts which, though necessarily detracting from the size of the auditorium, really add to its symmetry owing to the peculiar shape of the building. One shaft extends from the roof down behind the organ. The other two shafts are directly behind the two windows representing "Mary First at the Resurrection" and "Woman God-crowned," and the two smaller windows above them on the gallery level, thus brightening the pictured glass besides diffusing more light through the entire room. It was truly said that there had been brought to the church light from heaven, which no man could take away.

Still another feature adopted to secure more light as well as more beauty, was that of bronze window frames. The Romanesque style of architecture in which the church is built gives heavy walls and small openings. Heavy wooden casings would not only leave the windows too small for the best delineation of subjects in stained glass, but would also darken the interior somewhat; wooden frames were liable to rapid decay. After full discussion it was determined that all window casings should be of bronze, thus enlarging the area of glass in each window about six inches. Not knowing of any other building supplied with such frames, the contractor made original designs for them.

To secure uniformity of workmanship as well as harmony in color and style, the windows were all entrusted to the same Boston manufacturers. As the ideas of the designers were often far from the true interpretation of subjects to be brought out in the glazing, the presence of some Christian Scientist was required, who could be relied upon to watch the work daily. Such a person must be quick to catch the spiritual meaning of the Scripture to be illustrated or of the subject chosen to present the thought. This was not all, for skilled artisans would not willingly endure dictation from an outsider, and wisdom must be used or the workmen would refuse to proceed. The Directors wished to express in the designs the spiritual thoughts taught by Christian Science, while the artists attempted to follow traditional religious views as well as preconceived notions of art; and their material beliefs, inculcated by the popular theories of the day, constantly conflicted with the spiritual idea. One artist said, "I see that your windows *mean* something!" thus recognizing the difference between ordinary requirements and those now demanded.

A number of subjects were chosen by our teacher and

testimonial windows and other gifts

mother; others were selected by the donors or the Directors. The first one given as a testimonial was the rose window at the left of the platform, representing "The Raising of Jairus' Daughter," which was partly copied from a plate in one of the early editions of *Science and Health*. In the six lower sections, palms and lamps signify light, intelligence and victory.

The Directors' rose window, on the right side of the pulpit, was the next to be designed. In a conversation with our teacher and mother early in the summer she spoke of the four-sided city described by Saint John. As there were four Directors this suggested to them the idea of their giving the other rose window to the church and using "The New Jerusalem" as the theme. After careful study of the subject in connection with the beautiful spiritual interpretation of "the holy city, ... coming down from God out of heaven, prepared as a bride adorned for her husband," [1] the figures for the window were selected.

The definite outlines of the proposed window were not taken into consideration when this design from the Apocalypse was thought out, and the window had been planned without regard to any subject. Now, upon examination of the drawing, the Directors found a wonderful harmony between their ideas and the plan of the window.

This circular window was divided into two rows of twelve openings each; the outer panes separating the circle into segments, while each inner light had the shape of a keystone or sustaining wedge of an arch, sometimes supposed to be the stone designated by the psalmist as "the head stone of the corner." Twelve was a most significant number for the purpose; and, by dividing the segments into four groups of three each, there was one cluster to represent each side of the celestial city. In the central pane of each triplet was placed the main symbol of the group with explanatory figures in the two panes flanking it. The four main figures were the Bible, or Word of God; the Madonna and Child, representing Jesus;

[1] See *Science and Health with Key to the Scriptures*, p. 574.

the Southern Cross, standing for Christianity; the Golden Shore of Love, symbolizing Christian Science. In the twelve lights of the outer circle were as many stars, also arranged in four clusters of three lights each, one larger star and two smaller ones for each division.

The rounded central light was the proper place for an open *Science and Health with Key to the Scriptures.* This suggested the name "Window of the Open Book," signifying that the radiance from this new revelation shows the meaning of all the Bible promises and prophecies, as symbolized by the figures surrounding the center.

The architect's plan for this window further included six long lower lights which would come below the line of the gallery. The six water pots chosen for these places typify the six days of material creation included in the belief that man has a material origin and existence. They also call to memory the marriage in Cana with its spiritual lessons, teaching that, as mortals empty themselves of error through the understanding of Truth, they are being prepared for union with divine Principle, as shown in Christian Science.

This rose window has been symbolically read from top to bottom. Reversing this order the eye rises from the water pots, representing mortal consciousness, to rest upon the cross; then on, past *Science and Health,* to the topmost ring of lights, where the woman is standing upon the moon. So in our human experience: "We have this treasure in earthen vessels," as stated in II Corinthians 4:7; then we gradually rise by way of the cross till through Christian Science man as the divine idea of God is fully realized.

The other windows are here mentioned in their order of presentation. One of the finest in the church is a double window, "The Resurrection of Lazarus." Its rare perspective, made still more striking by the stone mullions and clasping irons, gives it an appearance of being outside the wall, as if one were gazing upon a scene of light and color beyond.

The designers wished to omit the wolf and the lamb from the Isaiah window in the vestibule, thinking that so many

Jesus with the Woman of Samaria

The Raising of Jairus' Daughter

Saint John on the Island of Patmos

Angel with the "little book"

Window of the Open Book

Woman God-crowned

Mary First at the Resurrection

Mary the Mother of Jesus

Mary Anointing the Head of Jesus

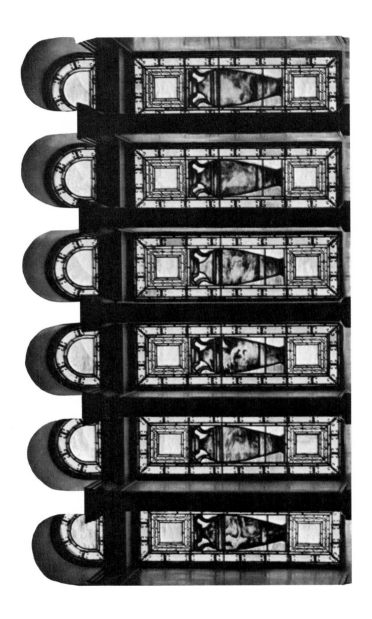

Earthen Vessels

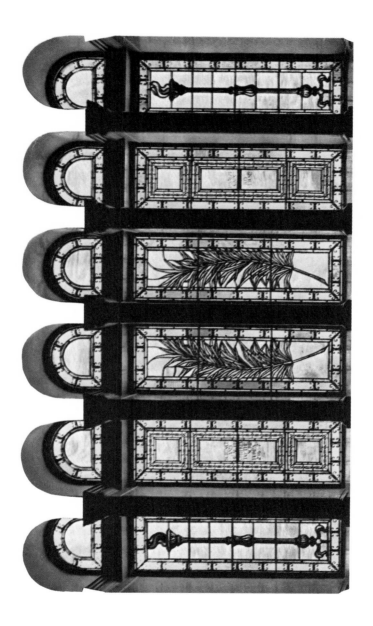

"Light, Intelligence and Victory"

Resurrection of Lazarus

"A Little Child Shall Lead Them"

figures would be inartistic, but when the spiritual meaning was explained they saw at once that these types were most necessary.

The design first submitted for the Apocalyptic angel with the "little book" represented the seraph as standing on what were intended for pillars of fire, but which looked like red bricks, and wearing materially feathered wings,—which useless appendages the artist could hardly be persuaded to eliminate.

Beside this window is portrayed Jesus with the woman of Samaria as he rested at Jacob's well.

"Saint John on the Island of Patmos," a double window, was copied from an Old Bible illustration.

Next in order came the left gallery window, painted with the Bible and *Science and Health.*

The four windows in the sides of the auditorium, representing subjects proposed by our teacher and mother, offer much food for thought. That of the Madonna and Jesus shows us woman's thought of God as the Father of all mankind, although expressed as yet in a feeble way. The next portrays woman anointing Jesus as the ideal man, who now expresses the thought of God's fatherhood in a still higher degree. "Mary First at the Resurrection" signifies that woman is first to perceive the risen man—that is, to recognize man as above and beyond what are called death and materiality. She has now faintly seen that man is spiritual, and Jesus gives her this message: "I ascend unto my Father, and your Father," [2] thus indicating the Master's recognition of her thought.

In a smaller window, above the Magdalene, is depicted an open Bible, whose record closes, as we know, with the prophecy of a God-crowned woman. This woman is the subject of the fourth window of the series, and above it, in a small separate window corresponding to the one where the Bible is painted, is another open volume, *Science and Health with Key to the Scriptures,* our textbook.

[2] John 20:17.

testimonial windows and other gifts

The woman of the Apocalypse and the teachings of Christian Science together signify that the perfect idea of God and the spiritual universe are revealed; that Christian Science, when understood, also reveals that the prophecy of Saint John is fulfilled and the spiritual idea is the God-crowned woman. In these windows the Bible and *Science and Health* are shown to be our true pastor and preacher, explaining the way of salvation to all mortals.

There is a peculiar circumstance connected with the arrangement of these windows. Placing them in their present order so that their story might be read from left to right, it was found that the infant Jesus had the best light; the "Anointing of Jesus" came in almost as good a place; the "Resurrection" window was rather dark; while the "God-crowned Woman," representing the highest revelation of all, had less light than any other window in the church. Thus we may see that while the human Jesus is recognized as the Son of God by many, the risen Christ, or the God-crowned ideal, is as yet but faintly seen.

"mother's room"

Jerusalem which is above is free, which is the mother of us all. — Galatians 4:26

Her children arise up, and call her blessed; . . . let her own works praise her in the gates. — Proverbs 31:28, 31

In the earliest church plans was included an apartment for the sole use of our beloved teacher and mother, Mrs. Eddy, to be known as "Mother's Room"; and soon after the building lot was deeded by her to the first board of trustees, the Christian Science children were organized into a band of Busy Bees, their special aim being the collection of money for this room. Chiefly through the efforts of its organizer, Miss Maurine R. Campbell, five thousand dollars were raised by this "sweet society."

In the early months it seemed as if this apartment must be finished and furnished very simply, as the Bees had gathered only a few hundred dollars, but November brought a different outlook. It was decided to appropriate the adjoining alcoves on either side for retiring rooms, and one beautiful idea followed another like the feet of messengers bringing good tidings to Zion. Very elaborate decorative designs were proposed but Mrs. Eddy desired that her room be adorned more simply and less expensively, though willing that its finishing should correspond with the rest of the building. The result could hardly be more harmonious or appropriate.

"mother's room"

The room is located on the auditorium stage of the tower and opens directly into the vestibule. The entrance as originally planned did not satisfy the Directors, and after several consultations the architect was requested to design a marble archway more in harmony with "Mother's Room." Early in December a plan was approved, and the marble, which was to be of the finest Italian, worked with great care, was ordered with the other marble.

In preparation, the opening for the doorway was widened on either side and the wall above cut out to the ceiling of the main vestibule, so that when the arch arrived the workmen began immediately to set it. The parties who took the contract for this work were very competent and had command of the best facilities. On a Friday, at six in the afternoon, the upright sections of the arch were in place to the finely carved cornice. To complete the task before Sunday seemed an impossibility, yet this was what those in charge had resolved upon. The workmen were asked how long it would take, and the reply was, "It is six days' work to set and finish the arch ready to fill in around it."

Arrangements were made with them to labor on continuously till the job was ended. The Scientists remained in the building that night to render all assistance possible, and a midnight meal was furnished the workmen. At six o'clock the next morning, in exactly twelve hours instead of six days, the arch was completed, and in an hour or two more the mason had filled in the wall around it with brick.

Two coats of plaster were then applied immediately to the newly set brickwork, and the painter followed with two coats of paint, matching perfectly the vestibuled walls which had been painted several days previously. This work was all done by six o'clock Saturday afternoon.

The archway leads by five marble steps into a small lobby, brightened by electric lamps artistically hidden behind the high cornice. The light illuminates the vaulted ceiling, and reflects a soft color from the rose tinted walls upon the white door with its golden knob. Above the door, in letters of gold on a white marble tablet, is the word LOVE. Near the ceiling on each side are three small stained glass casements, admitting enough light from two outside windows in the two dressing rooms to bring out the glazed colors and enhance the general effect. Inlaid with different colored stones in the mosaic landing before the door, may be read:

Mother's Room[1] The Children's Offering

The thoughts leading to these arrangements came one by one to the individual Scientists overseeing the work and seemed like inspirations from Love. Mrs. Eddy herself gave many helpful suggestions relative to all parts of the work, especially to decorations.

The following letter shows the source of two beautiful features connected with the entrance just described.

Pleasant View, Concord, N.H., Dec. 11, 1894.
Christian Science Directors:

My beloved Students,
Permit me to make this request relative to the Mother's Room, and if you think best grant it. On the marble floor at the entrance engrave the word, Mother; and on the arch above the word, Love.
Ever affectionately yours,
Mary Baker Eddy.

The apartment itself is fifteen feet in width and eighteen in length, measuring from the door to the middle of the bay. Here the first section of terra cotta flooring was laid. The room was plastered and painted before the tower was roofed, but it was protected from the weather by the bell deck, which had been covered with terra cotta, cement and ready roofing.

The baseboard, both for the main room and the adjacent dressing room, is of pure white Italian marble without dark veining. In the toilet room African marble, of Numidian red, is used alike for basin and baseboard, and the water-pipes are gold-plated.

[1] In 1904 in accordance with Art. XXII, Sect. 1, of the *Church Manual*, the title Mother's Room was changed in the mosaic to Rev. Mary B. Eddy's Room.

SCIENCE AND HEALTH
with Key to the Scriptures,
(THE CHRISTIAN SCIENCE TEXT-BOOK)
and other works,
by MARY BAKER G. EDDY.

Pleasant View,
CONCORD, N. H., Dec. 11.
1894.

Christian Science Directors:
My beloved Students,
Permit me to make this request relative to the Mother's Room, and if you think best grant it. On the marble floor at the entrance engrave the word, Mother; and on the arch above the word, Love.
Ever affectionately yours, Mary Baker Eddy.

Mrs. Eddy's letter of December 11, 1894

66

"mother's room"

The subjects for the three testimonial windows in "Mother's Room" are taken from *Christ and Christmas*, an illustrated poem by Mrs. Eddy. The "Star of Bethlehem" symbolizes the ray of Truth penetrating the darkness of mortal mind. "The light shineth in darkness; and the darkness comprehended it not"; [2] nevertheless it shines on, because it is from that divine source declared by Saint John to be "the life . . . of men." [3]

"Suffer Little Children to Come unto Me" represents the unbiased and innocent child-thought finding and appropriating the revelation of *Science and Health with Key to the Scriptures,* which explains the words and works of Jesus, the prophets and the apostles.

The face of the woman in the central window, "Seeking and Finding," is not a portrait of our teacher and mother but is a type which presents the thought of her, searching the Scripture with unalterable trust in the divine wisdom, above and beyond mortal concept. In this sacred search the "Star of Bethlehem," or gleam of Truth, is never lost sight of but shines steadily on the inspired page.

The last contract awarded was for the beautiful mantelpiece, constructed of onyx blocks from Puebla, Mexico, on exhibition at the World's Fair, Chicago, in 1893. Onyx of this opalescent green tint is said to be an object of worship with the Mexican Indians. Though this contract dated from only five days before Christmas, the mantel was in its place by New Year's.

Among the furnishings were many individual gifts. The rug before the fireplace, presented by a woman in the name of a child, was made by the Esquimaux from a hundred eider duck skins.

Other remembrances were an elaborately carved imported chair, an onyx table, a large china lamp and shade, the desk lamp shade, an Assyrian bridal veil, jardinière and cloisonné clock, two water colors by an English artist, valuable vases,

[2] John 1:5.
[3] v. 4.

Mother's Room — The Children's Offering
In late 1908 at Mrs. Eddy's request the room was closed
and furnishings removed

bookmarks and embroideries, a sofa pillow covered with white and gold tapestry, matching the other furniture, an Athenian hanging lamp two centuries old. Silvery green plush draperies and antique Persian rugs of similar tint harmonized with the delicate frescoing of the walls. A little onyx beehive contained the names of twenty-eight hundred Busy Bees. Everything was provided for the beloved mother's actual occupancy, as witness such tokens as a handkerchief, a tiny pincushion, dressing gown, slippers, and every needful toilet article.

Loving touches still continue to be added to this room, and ever will be, as long as hearts turn in gratitude to the one who gave her life for them and the world.

One of the latest additions was a gift from Mrs. Eddy herself to the church,—a large oil painting, measuring six feet by five, of the little rocking-chair, covered with black haircloth, in which she sat while writing *Science and Health*. It would seem impossible for such a room as this to afford space for so large a picture but the arrangement is so skillful as to increase the beauty of both. The picture rests on the floor and is lighted by electric lamps fastened on the upper edge of the frame and concealed by green draperies. The effect of the painting, so placed, is to enlarge as well as enrich the room for it is so realistic that, looking at it, one seems to be gazing into another apartment.

On a bookmark given by two little girls are printed some lines from Whittier which express the thought of many who enter this room:

And so I find it well to come,
For deeper rest, to this still room;
For here the habit of the soul

. . . .

Feels less the outer world's control;
And from the silence, multiplied
By these still forms on every side,
The world that time and sense has known
Falls off, and leaves us God alone.

the final effort

Be strong, . . . saith the Lord, and work: for I am with you. — Haggai 2:4
Behold, the tabernacle of God is with men, and he will dwell with them, and they shall be his people, and God himself shall be with them, and be their God. — Revelation 21:3

Mrs. Eddy's counsel was that the church should be in readiness for public service the last Sunday of the year 1894, as may be seen from the following letter:

Pleasant View, Concord, N.H., Dec. 19, 1894.

Christian Science Directors—

My beloved Students,
   The day is well nigh won. You will soon rest on your arms. Thank God you have been valiant soldiers—loyal to the heart's core. "Who is so great a God as our God?"
   Present no contribution box on Dedication day. When you know the amount requisite and have received it for finishing the church building—close all contributions and give public notice thereof.
   Hold your services in the Mother Church Dec. 30, 1894, and dedicate this church Jan. 6th. The Bible and *Science and Health with Key to the Scriptures* shall henceforth be the Pastor of the Mother Church. This will tend to spiritualize thought. Personal preaching has more or less of human views grafted into it. Whereas the pure Word contains only the living, health-giving Truth.
With love mother,

Mary Baker Eddy

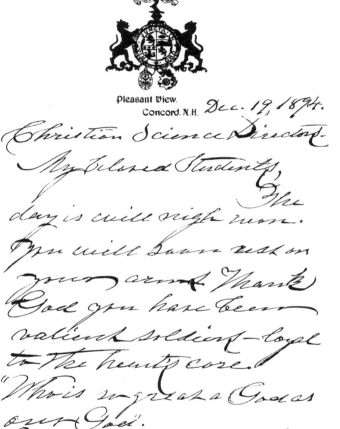

Pleasant View.
Concord. N.H. Dec. 19, 1894.

Christian Science Directors.
My Beloved Students,
The day is well nigh won. You will soon rest on your arms. Thank God you have been valiant soldiers—loyal to the heart's core. "Who is so great a God as our God".
Present no contribution boxes on Dedication day.

Mrs. Eddy's letter of December 19, 1894

71

P. 2

When you know the amount
requisite and have re-
ceived it for finishing
the church building —
close all contributions
and give public notice
thereof.

Hold your services in
the Mother church Dec. 30,
1894. and dedicate this church
Jan. 6th The Bible and
Science and Health with Key
To the Scriptures shall hence
forth be the Pastor of the
mother church. This will tend
to spiritualize thought. Personal preaching has more or less of
human hues grafted into it.
Whereas the word of God contains only
the living health giving Truth.
With love mother,
— Mary Baker Eddy

Mrs. Eddy's letter of December 19, 1894

72

the final effort

To have the building ready for use by December 30, a mighty effort must be made. Every part of the work must be pushed, and every moment of time utilized. Even then, to human sense the task seemed utterly hopeless. The decorating must be done, and platform and pulpit built. The gallery was as yet hardly begun, the vestry, "Mother's Room," vestibules, Directors' room and other sections of the edifice needed much more labor than seemed possible in ten days. Men must be kept busy every hour when work could be done, day and night. Work on the roof, tower, walls, stairways, metal window frames, glass, plastering, concrete, mosaic, woodwork, painting, marble work, wiring for electric lights, plumbing,—all must be pushed, and no one trade wait for another to move out of the way, if the building was to be used in 1894.

The marble, ordered December 6, had not yet reached Boston. On December 15, there was no one part of the church really completed except the walls; and ventilating flues had yet to be erected on these.

Every step up to this time had been made through demonstration of divine Science, the work of our beloved Leader. Not a point could be carried without her aid for she alone could show the way—God's way—and make it possible to do what mortal sense declared impossible. With this knowledge, those having the work in charge continued to press on in the face of all seeming discouragements, trusting Love to deliver them and enable the workmen to complete the building.

The work on the tower seemed very slow. A steam derrick had been hired to lift the stone and other material and a few days before the walls were finished the roofer tried to make a bargain for the use of this derrick to raise the heavy iron for the tower roof.

Confusion seemed to rise up among the men, and they were unable to come to any agreement on the matter. At this point Mrs. Bates was told of the situation and asked to see what could be done. She went at once in search of the man who controlled the derrick. He was at the top of the tower. Without hesitation she climbed up to find him, though this meant the ascent of three ladders, each one twenty or twenty-five feet long, set up on loose planks inside the tower wall.

This task was not only accomplished, but she made definite arrangements with the owner to let the derrick for one day to the Directors. The roofers were then notified to have their materials ready on the grounds, and on the appointed day all the iron for the frame and the terra cotta blocks were lifted to the tower platform, the slate and copper being hauled up later by hand.

Mrs. Bates also made a second trip to the bell deck within a few days, remaining there three hours in order to settle a dispute among the men and keep them at work.

With the masons there had already been some trouble on account of the irregularity of the contractors' payments, and now a new difficulty arose. In addition to the original contract, certain stones were to be removed from the top of the tower, so that the copper roof might be laid on the bell deck, and the stones then were to be put back in place. When the original contract was finished, the masons took out the stones as agreed, but refused to replace them. This was a genuine strike, for the men stayed around the place two or three days, not allowing others to finish the work. Tired of so thankless a job, however, they soon retired from the ground and gave no more trouble.

The first day, late in December, that the terra cotta was being laid in the iron frame of the tower roof was very cold and windy, especially at an altitude of a hundred and twenty feet above the level of the street. The Director who had especial charge of the building felt impelled to visit the seven men who were engaged in this work. He accordingly climbed the three ladders inside the tower to the bell deck, where he saw, swaying almost vertically above in the open belfry between him and the roof frame, a fourth ladder. This ladder was made of two scantlings which had been broken and patched, while several of the strips nailed crosswise for steps had been broken and left unrepaired. When the foot of this frail ladder was reached, seventy-five feet above the street, the Director's heart failed him, and he said to himself, "I cannot mount." Of course the workmen had used this same means to reach the roof, but they knew by experience what could be done and were used to such undertakings.

After a moment's silent prayer for strength from Mind, he slowly began the ascent. According to sense evidence the support appeared insufficient to bear his weight, with the wind blowing so fiercely through the arched openings of the tower, but he finally reached the roof. Here the wind blew stronger than ever, and it seemed impossible to hold on or even think. Again, in silent prayer and demonstration, harmony was realized and fears were overcome. The roofers were encouraged, and even the wind seemed to be quieter.

The Directors were obliged to look after each contractor to see that he fulfilled his engagements. More than this, they watched every workman lest in the rush some detail be slighted or hindrance arise, for well they knew not an hour could be lost.

The Italian mosaic layers, of whom there were separate gangs for dados, floors and borders, were perhaps the most troublesome to deal with because, as they spoke but little English, it was difficult to talk or reason with them. They were usually happy and good-natured, singing about their work, but if any one of them happened to be vexed he and his comrades would threaten to leave.

During the process of building a constant stream of students poured into the church, and every accessible part of the work was visited. This never disturbed the mechanics except in one instance, when, during the last week in December, some strangers stepped on a piece of mosaic bordering, just laid in soft mortar. The work was spoiled, and the Italian, muttering something in his own language, called his assistant and left the building, to be seen no more that day.

The contractor for stereo-relief moldings to be put on the

the final effort

gallery front and cornices had only nine days for his work; but he promised to have it done, or allow his unfinished moldings to be thrown into the street. Another contract remarkable for the short time in which it was fulfilled was that for the pulpit and for furniture in "Mother's Room," wherein the contractor agreed to have the articles ready in time or forfeit fifty dollars for every day's delay.

The pews were to come from Michigan by Christmas, but the agent, seeing the condition of the edifice in October, did not believe they would be wanted in December and inserted this clause in the contract, "by December 25th, *or as soon as the church is ready.*" When the Directors wrote to the manufacturers to hasten the work, they replied that the agent in Boston had informed them that the church would not be ready for two months. The Directors now saw, if the pews were to be in the building by December, that it would be necessary to send someone to the factory who would insist that the work be finished and delivered according to agreement.

Mr. James A. Neal was accordingly despatched to Michigan and when he explained the situation to the manufacturers they put all their force of workmen on this one job. Mr. Neal remained until the pews were made ready and then traced their course to Boston.

When the agent and the man who came from the factory to set up the pews entered the auditorium on Friday before Christmas and saw it full of workmen and scaffolding, they were alarmed for the carload of pews which could not be wisely left at the freight house, yet could not be set up in the church where there was not even room to store them.

That night the workmen stayed until morning, and students, both ladies and gentlemen, came in to help. The whole network of staging was taken down, the rough covering removed from the mosaic, and the floor washed.

When the Michigan man came in on Saturday morning he was astounded at the transformation. Even the architect, who had watched the progress of the work so closely, said that what had been accomplished that night seemed like a miracle. To make room for the seats, all the workmen had been cleared out except one who was fitting the capitals on the pillars. The pew agent refused to go to work until this mechanic was also sent away. No time could be lost in controversy, so the other artisans were recalled. On Monday he still refused to work, but on Tuesday he began setting up the pews while other men were busy in the room.

Tuesday was Christmas day, but the work continued as usual.

In order to have the exact shade of plush desired, the covering for the cushions had been ordered directly from Lyons, France. New York upholsterers had pledged themselves to have them ready by the middle of December. It was learned, however, that they had done nothing and would not, before January, so the plush was brought to Boston, and there the cushions were made ready in season.

It had been arranged to lay a sidewalk around the tower entrances; for, as the boiler-room would extend under this part of the walk, it was believed the heat would prevent the cement from freezing. The work was begun Friday, December 28. Saturday night it was not yet finished, and the weather had turned very cold, with a strong wind blowing. There was danger that the wet cement would freeze, and it seemed impossible to continue the work. The Directors hired a tent, and had it stretched over the walk and fastened to the church wall. The big doors were kept open, and all possible heat was secured from the boilers. The men worked until twelve o'clock, and then watched in the building till morning lest the canvas be blown down, but no injury came, and the sidewalk was ready for use the next day.

The same evening the church was full of students, dusting pews and sweeping floors, and exactly as the clock struck twelve, midnight, the auditorium was ready for Sunday. The first meeting, held December 30, 1894, was a communion service.

So, with the mother encouraging and pointing the way, and with divine Love sustaining, the church was built in the

Ready for services

appointed time, and the following notices appeared in the January issue of *The Christian Science Journal:*

Notice

The dedication services of the new building of The Mother Church, The First Church of Christ, Scientist, Boston, Massachusetts, will be held on the first Sunday in January, the sixth, 1895. An address from our former pastor, the Rev. Mary Baker Eddy, will be read, but she will not be present at these services. Christian Science Board of Directors.

A Card from Mr. Chase

As treasurer of the Christian Science Board of Directors, I hereby return sincere thanks to all the donors to the church building fund of The Mother Church, for their most generous contributions, and their prompt responses to all calls sent out. There are ample funds now in my hands to meet all obligations, and all contributions should cease after January 6, 1895, as none can be received which were not subscribed prior to that date.

Stephen A. Chase,
Treasurer.

The last card suggests the following incident from Biblical history:

And they spake unto Moses, saying, The people bring much more than enough for the service of the work, which the Lord commanded to make. And Moses gave commandment, and they caused it to be proclaimed throughout the camp, saying, Let neither man nor woman make any more work for the offering of the sanctuary. So the people were restrained from bringing. For the stuff they had was sufficient for all the work to make it, and too much.
Exodus 36:5-7.

conclusion

Let us hear the conclusion of the whole matter: Fear God, and keep his commandments: for this is the whole duty of man. — Ecclesiastes 12:13

To material sense and according to the evidence cognizable thereby man is material with but a vague perception, if any at all, of Spirit and spiritual law. The aim of Christian Science is to show mortals the way out of this false and therefore unreal condition. Science must control every human experience until all is brought into complete subjection to Spirit.

Mortals allow this control and yield to God's government only as they are driven to distrust and doubt the evidence of the material senses, thus becoming willing to abandon these senses and accept and adopt the evidence of Spirit. This usually comes through suffering. First, we allow Christian Science to heal us of physical pain; then, when we have learned something of its teachings, our old theology begins to disappear. As false theories about God and man are dispelled through understanding what God is and man's relation to Him, we begin to see the true nature of sin and how to overcome its claims.

To say that we see this to be true, and accept it as a theory, is not enough. It must be proven by demonstration, and this demonstration must be that which will reach the human consciousness on the plane of its own experiences. If a man is in a pit a hundred feet deep, a rope ninety feet long, though held above by strong and loving hands, can be of no practical benefit to him. This illustrates the impotence of theories in regard to an unknown God and a far-away heaven to be obtained only through death and a personal Saviour.

So, in the history of the spiritualization of human consciousness, the thought of church must be discerned spiritually and yet so manifested that it can be recognized by mortals. Christian Science had proven itself a healer of the sick and now it must show itself the destroyer of false theorems and sin.

When the children of Israel started for the promised land, no doubt they expected to have an easy time as soon as they had turned their backs on their enemies, but in a very short while they found themselves pursued by their foes, and further progress cut off by barriers seemingly insurmountable. Moses, reflecting more of God than his countrymen, bade them, "Stand still, and see the salvation of the Lord." [1] That is, they were to see a demonstration of the power of Mind over matter, of Truth over error.

In building The Mother Church, to stand as a symbol of all the teachings of Christian Science and of all that Christianity implies, the Directors found themselves in a position similar to that of the Israelites when behind them was Pharaoh's army and in front of them the Red Sea.

A great struggle was inevitable. Every material help was withheld until divine Love was sufficiently reflected to meet the opposing error in all its various forms and turn the scale on the side of God and His government. The spirituality and divinity of Christian Science is proven when we learn that it is opposed by all materiality.

A few thousand dollars were raised by great human effort, and land on which to erect a building purchased; but as the money was lost, and the lot about to be sold under foreclosure of mortgage, failure seemed inevitable. Yet this was not true. The one chosen of God to lead mortals out of this

[1] Ex. 14:13.

81

dream of sin and death was not forsaken, but was shown the way to save the land by herself paying the cost, thus bringing victory out of seeming defeat.

Again money was solicited from the students to build a church on this same lot, now in the hands of trustees for this purpose. As soon as enough money was received so that the work might have been begun, a question arose which checked further progress in this direction. Once more error was defeated, the lot was deeded to another board under new and wiser provisions, and the money returned to a new treasurer.

Then came the announcement that the building should be finished in 1894 and the awful struggle,—that is, awful to human sense,—began. Every step must be demonstrated. Error was, or seemed to be, in possession and would yield only as Truth and Love were manifested. Every law of matter seemed opposed. There was lack of means, time was passing, and every human effort proved ineffective. November came, and found no roof on the building, the walls unfinished and snow already on the ground. There were even no suitable plans for interior finish and but two months in which to complete work that all agreed would require at least six. Yet these difficulties, so insurmountable to the human sense, were as nothing when weighed in the balance with the unchanging demand of Love that the work should be finished within the time specified.

It might be asked in this case, as in that of the children of Israel: Did God plan that these innocent and confiding people should come into such difficulties, merely to show His power in leading them out? This could never be true of divine wisdom.

The truth is, that as mortals learn something of the nature of evil and make efforts to overcome it, they are then met by its different forms, resisting the demands of good. Then evil shows its true nature by claiming to be something when it is really nothing. The building of this church was to be a

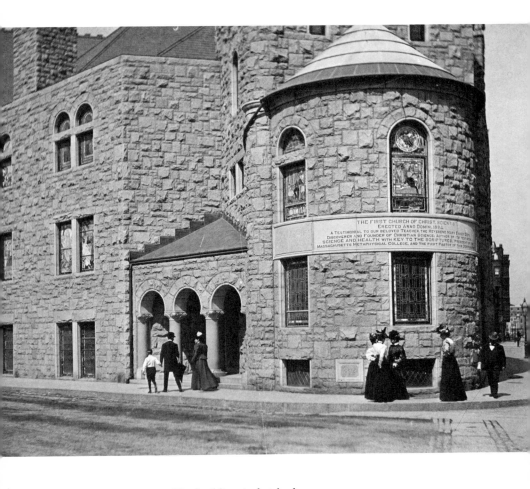

The building is finished

triumph for divine Love, and every material means and human dependence must fail, for human sense must "stand still, and see the salvation of the Lord." [2]

Nothing but the hand of divine wisdom could have guided and upheld those entrusted with this responsibility through such a trial of faith as this was. Neither could they have had this divine assistance but for the nearness to God of the "mother in Israel," which gave her counsel to reflect the one omnipotent Mind to those charged with this great work for God and humanity.

It was a victory for Christian Science, a victory in which every claim of error was met and overcome. Something was accomplished which must be accepted by mortals as a part of the world's history. The fair and impartial accounts of the church, given by the press at the time of the dedication, illustrate this point. Just as a large part of mankind have accepted the lives of Jesus and his apostles as historic facts, however little this may affect their own living; just as proofs of astronomical facts, reversing the evidence of the senses, are universally undenied,—so the erection of this church is so great a demonstration of Christianity and Science as to leave on the world's thought an indelible mark which must be given a place in its history.

Only future ages can fully appreciate and understand the mighty triumph of good over evil, of Spirit over matter, manifested in the circumstances connected with the successful erection of this beautiful building, as given in this historical sketch of The Mother Church in Boston.

[2] Ex. 14:13.

the financial question in Christian Science

From my earliest recollection, when reading the Bible stories of the patriarchs, their success in accumulating an abundance of this world's goods was a source of wonder and speculation as to the reason of their being thus specially favored. Since gaining some knowledge of Christian Science I have learned that it was not because they were specially favored by a personal God, but because of their better acquaintance with and consciousness of true relationship to the one true God. This was beautifully illustrated in the incident recorded when Elisha fed the vast number of people with barley loaves and full ears of corn, and all did eat and much remained thereof. [1]

In metaphysics we learn that the human mind is an idolater, attributing all cause and effect and all law to matter, thus enthroning matter as God, and seeming to expect thereby to shirk all responsibility for its own falsity. The human mind claims these laws of matter can cause man to be sick and die. It has made money to be the standard and to determine the value of all things. Paul says "the love of money is the root of all evil," [2] meaning thereby that one who accepts this standard of values partakes of the very essence of mortal mind delusion.

[1] See II Kings 4:42-44.
[2] I Tim. 6:10.

the financial question in Christian Science

It is often said of Jesus that he was poor so far as material goods were concerned. But was this true? He said of himself, "Foxes have holes, and birds of the air have nests; but the Son of man hath not where to lay his head." [3] No doubt Jesus saw that the sensuous age in which he lived would not receive his teachings. Even those he selected as students were not ready to receive all of his teachings. He said, "I have yet many things to say unto you, but ye cannot bear them now." [4] For this reason he could impart his knowledge of God to but a few humble followers. The final establishment of his teaching must come at a later period when the world would be more ready to receive it.

Although he recognized the inability of his students to receive all of his teachings, he knew the time was coming when they would be received and understood; hence he promised the Comforter that should lead "into all truth." [5] This seems a reasonable explanation of why our beloved Master "went about all the cities and villages, teaching . . . preaching the gospel . . . and healing," [6] rather than establishing himself in a local habitation. But we cannot believe this Man of God, who wore the beautiful seamless garment, unto whom people freely gave of their substance out of gratitude for the healing he had done for them, ever really lacked the material needs and comforts; to say nothing of his ability to feed the multitudes, as recorded of him. [7]

In Christian Science we learn that Spirit is substance, and alone has value or can give value. We reflect this value in proportion as we understand and reflect Spirit. We are enabled to rob matter of its claims of power and to see and handle it as a mere belief or delusion. This is what I understand is meant by establishing "the kingdom of God, and his righteousness."

[3] Luke 9:58.
[4] John 16:12.
[5] See John 16:7-13.
[6] Matt. 9:35.
[7] See Matt. 14:17-20.

the financial question in Christian Science

When the writer first became interested in Christian Science, he lost all interest in business the object of which was moneymaking. He did not understand the reason for this at that time, but subsequent experience and his growth in Christian Science have taught him that the only real value is Spirit—God; that when we reflect the true substance in our daily lives, our daily needs, both temporal and spiritual, will be bountifully supplied. Christian Science is this Comforter, and has come through the revelation of our beloved Leader, Mary Baker Eddy.

This chapter is written, not for those Scientists who have learned by their own experience and growth in Christian Science how to meet this question, but with a hope that it may help those who must come face to face with this problem of finance, which has caused young students so many bitter struggles.

Joseph Armstrong

The Extension

preface

The purpose of this little book is transparently simple. Since Christian Scientists have long profited by the spiritual inspiration found in Mr. Joseph Armstrong's THE MOTHER CHURCH, it has been felt that one day there should be a companion volume dealing with its Extension. Hence the request of the Board of Trustees of The Christian Science Publishing Society that such a book be prepared.

The author is well aware that probably no one today, certainly not herself, is in a position to bring to this task the comprehension which Mr. Armstrong brought to his; for Mr. Armstrong was himself intimately concerned with the struggles and the triumphs encountered by that small band of Mrs. Eddy's followers engaged in the erection of the Original Church. When the Extension was under consideration, all the attendant circumstances were vastly altered. By this time, there were many more students to support the activities of those who directed the momentous task.

According to her own highest light, the author has described the progress of events—from the moment when it was resolved to build the Extension, through the months of its erection, on to the "crowning glory" of its completion and dedication. The mere contemplation of the accomplishment of this mighty task, carried out under Mrs. Eddy's guidance and in the light of spiritual understanding, cannot but be fraught with profound import for all Christian Scientists.

Margaret Williamson

need for expansion

The great gray form of The Mother Church Extension is to-day a recognized landmark in Boston, long the headquarters of the Christian Science movement. Local residents have come to take its presence for granted. Affectionately, perhaps sometimes a trifle wonderingly, they glance up at it in passing; streetcar conductors refer to it familiarly, and innumerable sightseeing omnibuses include it in their tours of inspection. At night the floodlights directed upon the dome cause it to be visible—all silver-white and shining—from far out across the dim reaches of the Fenway. For a number of years now, it has risen in its chosen place, which is today flanked by the Administration Building and the Christian Science Publishing House on two sides, [1] on the third side by the friendly park with its wide inviting paths leading to Huntington Avenue.

However, this building is much more than merely the largest church in the city of Boston; for it stands a revered and significant witness to the faith of thousands of Christian Scientists all over the world. It cannot be dismissed in any peremptory fashion, since every step in its inception and erection becomes important and worthy of careful reflection.

Mary Baker Eddy, in the Message which was read to her followers on the occasion of the dedication of this Extension of The First Church of Christ, Scientist, in Boston, June 10,

[1] Written some years before completion of the Christian Science Center in 1975.

need for expansion

1906, refers to that edifice as "a magnificent temple wherein to enter and pray." [2] The phrase leaves no room for doubt that within her vision of the building's true import existed no element of pride in materiality. It was matter of secondary moment that the new church embodied a might, a majesty, and a grace far beyond the bounds ordinarily achieved by a church body seeking to erect a suitable place in which to conduct its worship. These characteristics were but the natural outward expression of an inward devotion, consecration, and development.

Thus it becomes strikingly impressive to dwell upon the purpose and function of The Mother Church Extension, as set forth by the Discoverer and Founder of Christian Science. In the same Message she writes: "The modest edifice of The Mother Church of Christ, Scientist, began with the cross; its excelsior extension is the crown. . . . Its crowning ultimate rises to a mental monument, a superstructure high above the work of men's hands, even the outcome of their hearts, giving to the material a spiritual significance—the speed, beauty, and achievements of goodness. Methinks this church is the one edifice on earth which most prefigures self-abnegation, hope, faith; love catching a glimpse of glory." [3]

Anyone who would know more of the human processes which went into the building of the Extension must desire at the same time to keep uppermost in his thought its spiritual counterpart, that "mental monument" which Mrs. Eddy beheld.

Often it is helpful to think back a little, thus to catch up the threads and gain a clearer sense of the pattern woven entire. From the autumn of 1882 to June of 1883, Mrs. Eddy's followers held their meetings in the parlors of her home at 569 Columbus Avenue, Boston. Then after an interval, more space being urgently required, the services were resumed at the Hawthorne Rooms on Park Street which accommodated about two hundred and twenty-five persons. There

[2] *The First Church of Christ, Scientist, and Miscellany*, p. 6.
[3] *ibid.*, p. 6.

93

Mrs. Eddy's sermons attracted more and more inquirers into Christian Science until, at the February communion service of 1885 in Odd Fellows Hall, there were about eight hundred in attendance. Finally, matters having reached a pass where, Sunday after Sunday, the crowds increased perceptibly, it was decided to engage Chickering Hall on Tremont Street. This latter hall could accommodate four hundred and sixty-four persons, yet at the first Sunday service held therein the hall was overcrowded.

It was self-evident that the Christian Scientists must have an edifice of their own, and negotiations were in progress for the purchase of land upon which a building might be erected. In March, 1894, Chickering Hall had become so crowded that another removal was made—this time to Copley Hall on Clarendon Street, where six hundred persons might comfortably congregate. There the services were held until the Original Mother Church Edifice was ready on December 30, 1894. That church seats just under a thousand persons. Many supposed it would suffice for years to come, and astonishment was general when the attendance so increased that, by April, 1896, it was necessary to hold two services each Sunday, and by October, 1905, three.

Still the evidence was of the ever-growing number of those who sought the healing ministrations of Christian Science. In larger and larger throngs they presented themselves at the doors, until not alone every seat was taken, but people stood in the rear of the auditorium, they stood at the front near the Readers' platform, they stood in the balcony, they sat on the stairs and on the wide ledges of the windows. No one who was privileged to be present on such occasions will ever forget the eagerness, the spiritual hunger of those who so crowded the church, the fresh and compelling quality of the appeal. At that time people still rented their own pews and, though their families commonly filled them, yet it was often possible to find space for one person more. That was preeminently a time for sharing the new wonder of the vision of Truth.

need for expansion

Perhaps simplicity and genuineness, sincerity, and self-sacrifice were the qualities most conspicuous in the lives of these early followers of Mrs. Eddy. Nothing was too much for them to do in return for the spiritual benefits received. To one woman there remained very little of material worth except a pair of diamond earrings. Very well; she would give those—her all. Such sharing, such consecration! Here was a new way of life; for a standard had been lifted up, and these men and women set about to attain it by the regeneration of their own characters. They were hungry for Truth. As yet there were no lectures; hence people flocked ever more and more eagerly to the services. Healings were reported from one to another. With their own eyes, people witnessed such marvelous healings that they could no longer feel doubt in their hearts. Had they not seen one man gain release from a physical disability which had bent his body almost double, so that he could not stand upright? Sunday after Sunday he came to the services, being helped off the streetcar by his family and proceeding slowly and painfully to the church, carrying on his arm a little folding chair on which he sat down frequently to rest. Little by little he improved; first, he needed no help from others, then he walked without the folding stool and, finally, he stood erect and rejoicing like the rest. Many noticed and were grateful. More and more of them hurried to the services and knew a deep joy in the realization that this was their church of which they might become members.

In the hearts of those who attended services in the Original Mother Church lingered always the hope that Mrs. Eddy might come to speak to them there. Twice, indeed, it happened even as they hoped. On one occasion a sudden hush fell in the midst of the service as the voice of Judge Septimus J. Hanna, who was then First Reader, broke off; then the organ pealed in response to a quick signal. And those who turned their heads saw Mrs. Eddy standing on the threshold of one of the rear doors, escorted by one of her students. A few seconds she halted there, prayerfully; then quickly, lightly, a radiant smile on her face, she moved down the left aisle to be received by Judge Hanna and escorted to her chair on the platform. Twice Mrs. Eddy spoke from that platform, and those who were fortunate enough to be present treasure an unforgettable impression of the sacredness of the occasion.

While these experiences were taking place, the more alert of the workers had foreseen that things could not continue as they were. Some provision had to be made for the increasing hosts who desired to attend this church regularly. Accordingly three branch churches were organized at Mrs. Eddy's direction: in Cambridge, in Chelsea, and in Roxbury. It was thought they would attract some of the eager throngs; and so they did, but not to the extent of preventing the overcrowded conditions in Boston. More and more persons came. Anyone might detect the increase in their numbers from week to week. Some further step needed to be taken; indeed, a larger edifice had become an absolute necessity. The Original Church, with all its precious import, had definitely become inadequate to receive all who desired to attend its services.

It can be shown that already in June, 1896, only eighteen months after the Original Mother Church had been finished, Mrs. Eddy was thinking of the next step. There is extant a message from her, dictated in that month and recording her belief that it would be unwise to pay out a certain sum of money, then under consideration, for such provision as would seat only eight hundred more persons in the auditorium. In August, 1901, there was a plan for the purchase of the Hotel Brookline, a four-story brick building which occupied a part of the triangular plot of land which the church eventually bought in 1903 and upon which the Extension was built. That project would, it was thought, afford opportunity to enlarge the Original Church until it would seat five thousand persons; but in those days the church treasury was meager. Indeed, in September of 1901, Mrs. Eddy again advised the church members that neither the Hotel Brookline

need for expansion

nor other properties should be bought until the church had more abundant funds at its disposal.

As always, Mrs. Eddy's followers waited for some action on the part of their Leader. This they did spontaneously and in all humility and willingness, for it was right that the initiative for any further step in progress should be hers. Sometimes it seemed to them that they waited a long time; but in this case it was not so. For Mrs. Eddy's Message to the church for June, 1902, made known her belief that a larger church building was needed immediately. She wrote thus in part: "Here allow me to interpolate some matters of business that ordinarily find no place in my Message. It is a privilege to acquaint communicants with the financial transactions of this church, so far as I know them, and especially before making another united effort to purchase more land and enlarge our church edifice so as to seat the large number who annually favor us with their presence on Communion Sunday." [4] Nothing more was required to insure that "united effort" to which Mrs. Eddy referred; she had only to give the signal for advance.

[4] *Miscellany*, p. 7.

a commitment to build

The Annual Meeting of June, 1902, marks the real beginning. It was then that The Mother Church Extension was born in purpose of fulfillment.

For want of an adequate building of their own, the church members had resolved to hold their business meeting in Mechanics' Hall on Boston's Huntington Avenue. That day the vast place seemed transformed; it had become suddenly and vibrantly alive, even gay, its ranks upon ranks of uncushioned seats crowded with enthusiastic Christian Scientists from all over the United States and other lands. The hot sun glinted upon their light summer garments, as fans and programs fluttered to supplement the faint breeze entering at the high windows. A small army of ushers moved up and down the aisles—young men who were faithful followers of the teachings of Christian Science. On the distant platform were gathered those who were to take a prominent part in the proceedings. Judge and Mrs. Hanna were present, of course, Judge William G. Ewing, too, and Mr. Edward A. Kimball, as well as others no less devoted and loyal. The strong voices of the congregation filled the great hall to its rafters as they sang the hymns; and somehow, miraculously, in an age when loudspeakers had not yet been introduced, it was possible to hear individual speakers on the platform when they rose to give their addresses.

All was as usual until, in the course of the program, there

a commitment to build

occurred a sudden pause after which rose Mr. Kimball, one of Mrs. Eddy's students, who offered the following resolution: "Recognizing the necessity for providing an auditorium for The Mother Church that will seat four or five thousand persons, and acting in behalf of ourselves and the Christian Scientists of the world, we agree to contribute any portion of two million dollars that may be necessary for this purpose. . . . Our denomination is palpably outgrowing the institutional end thereof. We need to keep pace with our own growth and progress. The necessity here indicated is beyond cavil; beyond resistance in your thought." [1]

Mr. Kimball was right in anticipating no resistance. While those who composed the audience had, for the most part, no previous knowledge of this motion which had just been made, there was manifest in their response neither doubt nor hesitation. In every respect it was a joyous meeting; the church members were happy and confident. The new revelation of Truth was fresh and replete with promise, and here was only one more challenge to command their grateful response.

There may perhaps have been a quick pause for breath, then a whisper of startled awe as the people caught the phrase "any portion of two million dollars." And this murmur and stir of enthusiasm had scarcely subsided when Judge Ewing took the floor, alert to second Mr. Kimball's motion. "As we have the best church in the world," said Judge Ewing, "and as we have the best expression of the religion of Jesus Christ, let us have the best material symbol of both of these, and in the best city in the world. Now I am sure that I have but expressed the universal voice of Christian Scientists, that there should be something done, and done immediately, to make reasonable accommodation for the regular business of the Christian Science church, and I believe really" (and here crept into Judge Ewing's voice that spark of humor which his friends so delight to remember), "with my faint knowledge of arithmetic and the relationship

[1] *Miscellany*, pp. 7–8.

of figures, that a church of twenty-four thousand members should have a seating capacity of more than nine hundred, if they are all   get in." [2]

The argument was as unanswerable as it was humorous. Once put to the vote, the motion was carried unanimously and every person present must have been persuaded in his own mind that two million dollars would be available when desired. Later in the course of that memorable Annual Meeting, the ten thousand Christian Scientists assembled sent a greeting to their Leader, Mrs. Eddy, making allusion to the motion which had just been carried with such enthusiasm and confidence.

Inevitably, and with utter conviction, it was felt that the pledge was so relatively slight a return for the blessings received through the study of the teachings of Christian Science, that it would unquestionably be made good. Yet Mrs. Eddy did not lose a shade of the significance of that magnificent gesture. Her letter of thanks to the members of The Mother Church, dated at Pleasant View, Concord, New Hampshire, was written on July 21, 1902. "I am bankrupt in thanks to you, my beloved brethren, who at our last annual meeting pledged yourselves with startling grace to contribute any part of two millions of dollars towards the purchase of more land for its site, and to enlarge our church edifice in Boston. I never before felt poor in thanks, but I do now, and will draw on God for the amount I owe you, till I am satisfied with what my heart gives to balance accounts." [3]

No time was lost in making plans for the project. The first consideration was, of course, the land on which The Mother Church Extension should be built. So, slowly and with cautious forethought, in obedience to their Leader's injunction that ideals of economy and order should be applied to all human situations, it was necessary to buy up a number of properties in the vicinity. Only certain of these properties along Norway, Falmouth, and St. Paul streets then belonged to the

[2] *Miscellany,* p. 8.
[3] *Ibid.,* p. 9.

church, so first one, then another, whether brick building, dwelling house, or the Hotel Brookline, had to be purchased. Sometimes this business was transacted in the name of a private individual and occasionally the purchaser lived in the house, thus naturally and unobtrusively making sure that it would remain in the control of the church. All this was matter for painstaking procedure, undertaken with tact and patience; until finally, in April, 1903, the purchase of the necessary land, comprised in the triangular-shaped lot which had once included in all ten separate lots, was complete. Then the church owned the whole of the block, bordered by Falmouth, Norway, and St. Paul streets, on one corner of which stood already the Original Mother Church.

In the issue of the *Christian Science Sentinel* for May 16, 1903, appeared two important articles which were concerned with the progress of the work for the Extension. They apprised the members of the church all over the world that the land for the new building had been purchased and paid for—that the location was, therefore, determined. They reminded the members of the pledge for the raising of the necessary money which had been approved at the preceding Annual Meeting. Then it was stated definitely that work would begin just as soon as the requisite funds were in hand; that is to say, it would begin at any time after the Annual Meeting of 1903, Mrs. Eddy having stipulated that nothing should be done before that time. The articles, which may now be read in *The First Church of Christ, Scientist, and Miscellany,* went on to make it clear that the time was ripe for the entire sum of money to be made available; and they stated plainly that, in accordance with the practice adhered to generally by Christian Scientists, no appeal for this money would be made. Quietly, confidently, it was pointed out that Christian Scientists would obey the dictates of their own grateful hearts, as they invariably had done in circumstances of the sort. No Christian Scientist who had the welfare of the Cause in mind would fail to realize the importance of this building of The Mother Church Extension.

a commitment to build

Further, the editorials showed that no such step as the erection of a new church had been contemplated until such a time as Mrs. Eddy "knew that we were ready." "We know that in all this time she has never urged upon us a step that did not result in our welfare. A year ago she quietly alluded to the need of our Mother Church. She knew that we were ready; the response was instant, spontaneous. Later on she expressed much gratification because of prompt and liberal action, and it needs no special insight to predict that she will be cheered and encouraged to know that, having seized upon this privilege and opportunity, we have also made good the pledge." [4]

After that it was necessary only to await results, for Christian Scientists have ever been quick to grasp an opportunity to express their gratitude by serving their Cause; as to the amount and the promptness of the contributions made, they had only to work out such conditions in accordance with the promptings of their own conscience. If other impetus had been required to stir her followers to action, it would have been found in Mrs. Eddy's article, "Now and Then," published first in the *Christian Science Sentinel* for May 30, 1903, and appearing today in *The First Church of Christ, Scientist, and Miscellany.* Every Christian Scientist is familiar with the inspiring words of this message; for its spirit is applicable, not alone to the momentous project of the erection of a church edifice, but to every least problem which presents itself in the human experience of the individual church member.

So, at this time as at many other times, it was proved that Christian Scientists have only to be apprised that a need exists in order to rise up at once to fill it. Perhaps better than most people they recognize the inexpressible blessing that results from acting generously, freely, at the precise moment when their action is desired; acting *now* and not *then.* The problem of raising the funds for The Mother Church Extension proved no exception to the rule. The money began to flow into the church coffers.

[4] *Miscellany*, p. 11.

the building begins

Although The Mother Church Extension building fund was declared at the beginning of the year 1904 to be "in such a healthy state that building operations have been commenced," [1] yet after the actual work was begun vast sums of money were required constantly. In a manner of speaking, the progress of the work depended upon the rapidity with which the church members responded in support of the project. It was indeed necessary at one time to correct an impression which had somehow got abroad that The Mother Church building fund was oversubscribed. An editorial in the *Christian Science Sentinel* for January 2, 1904, called attention to the subtlety of this suggestion and affirmed reassuringly that building operations would be carried on without interruption until the church was finished; but it included, too, a reminder that "the building fund [must] keep pace with the disbursements." [2]

Plans for the layout of the building were in preparation, work upon them having been protracted over a period of about six months, that is to say, the latter half of the year 1903. The architects considered structures of diverse character and form; they even contemplated various measures for the extension of the plot of land itself into that portion of the property now occupied by the church park. The plans were

[1] *Miscellany*, p. 14.
[2] *Ibid.*

Site of the Extension in 1895

the building begins

made in a city office; but, when they were nearing completion, the architect, his chief assistant, and an office force of about a dozen draftsmen and clerks established themselves in a temporary building adjacent to what has now become the church park. Thereafter all work was done upon the premises, those in charge being in close touch with the work by day, and often by night as well.

All digging was done "by hand" and the material hoisted laboriously into carts to be carried away; and yet rapid progress was made even without many of the modern devices which would today enter into such a building project. The site, too, was a difficult one because, as was common in the Back Bay section of Boston, it was what is called "filled land," marshy and affected by tidewater. For this reason, it was necessary to drive a stout foundation of piles. In all more than four thousand wooden piles were driven, their heads twelve feet below the level of the sidewalk, their tips firmly embedded in solid ground. In places the piles were driven so close that they formed practically a compact mass. It may be interesting to record that the plot of ground comprised an area of 33,200 square feet within the property limits. The plot is of extremely irregular outline, having eight major angles and a number of minor ones where the new building joined the old. There are no parallel lines. Indeed the shape of the plot has been described as a twisted hourglass, pinched in the center with its swelling ends bent sidewise. It is very long on St. Paul Street, approximately 256 feet from one sharply angled corner to the other; but a relatively small space was available in the center. Because of all these unusual characteristics, the task of drawing the building plans took on an extraordinary difficulty. About a hundred and fifty sketches were produced in those six months during which the design of the building was coming into being. The question of resorting to some device for extending the limits of the plot of land having been abandoned, it became necessary to create the illusion of great open spaces around the future structure whereas, in actuality, the corners of the church edifice were forced to be set to the very limits of the lot. But the decision had been irrevocable that the Extension should be contiguous to the Original Church, no matter how many obstacles there were to overcome.

A number of positions for the placing of the cornerstone were considered, but final choice fell upon that at the corner of St. Paul and Falmouth streets; a great block was cut and its face inscribed with the date 1904. Early on the morning of July 16, of that same year, the cornerstone of the new auditorium was laid. At eight o'clock few persons were about; and for this reason the members of The Christian Science Board of Directors, Mr. Alfred Farlow, President of The Mother Church, Professor Hermann S. Hering, who was its First Reader, and Mrs. Ella E. Williams, who was its Second Reader, together with Mr. Charles Brigham, who was its architect, and Mr. E. Noyes Whitcomb, its builder, came together then for the simple ceremony.

Professor Hering read selections from the Bible and from *Science and Health with Key to the Scriptures,* which selections had been chosen by the Board of Directors and approved by Mrs. Eddy. Extracts were read also from other writings by Mrs. Eddy, from *Miscellaneous Writings* and from *Christian Science versus Pantheism,* all bearing upon the true meaning of church and the proper conduct of its functions. When the cornerstone itself was put in place by the members of The Christian Science Board of Directors, the stone contained the following books and articles: the Holy Bible; *Science and Health with Key to the Scriptures* and all other published writings of Mary Baker Eddy, the Discoverer and Founder of Christian Science; *Christian Science Hymnal; The Mother Church,* by Joseph Armstrong; current numbers of *The Christian Science Journal, Christian Science Sentinel, Der Herold der Christian Science,* and the *Christian Science Quarterly.* The ceremony was concluded with the repetition of "the scientific statement of being" from *Science and Health,* and the benediction from

the building begins

II Corinthians 13:14: "The grace of the Lord Jesus Christ, and the love of God, and the communion of the Holy Ghost, be with you all. Amen."

After these simple ceremonies, the summer sun having risen higher and the activities of the day being under way, the little band of Christian Scientists dispersed to take up their several tasks. The work of erecting The Mother Church Extension was formally under way.

That every contribution to the new church, made unselfishly by an individual church member or by a branch church membership collectively, was appreciated by Mrs. Eddy is evidenced in a letter which she addressed to one of the many branch churches which sent in its own building fund to swell The Mother Church fund—First Church of Christ, Scientist, of Colorado Springs, Colorado. Mrs. Eddy wrote in part: "It is conceded that our shadows follow us in the sunlight wherever we go; but I ask for more, even this: That this dear church shall be pursued by her *substance*, the immortal fruition of her unselfed love, and that her charity, which 'seeketh not her own' but another's good, shall reap richly the reward of goodness.

"Those words of our holy Way-shower, vibrant through time and eternity with acknowledgment of exemplary giving, no doubt fill the memory and swell the hearts of the members of The Mother Church, because of that gift which you so sacredly bestowed towards its church building fund." [3]

Great reward did, indeed, overtake such donors to The Mother Church building fund. The money continued to come and, correspondingly, there continued always the need for more money to keep pace with the rapidly developing work. At Mrs. Eddy's request, those who contemplated giving holiday gifts to her at the Christmas season of 1904 sent instead "all [their] tithes into His storehouse," [4] into The Mother Church building fund. In May, 1905, appeared a "Word from the Directors" in which it was shown that there

[3] *Miscellany*, p. 19.
[4] *Ibid.*, p. 20.

the building begins

was urgent need for the building fund to be completed as early as possible; and, accordingly, those church members who would under ordinary circumstances have traveled to Boston to attend The Mother Church communion service and the Annual Meeting of June, 1905, were asked instead to contribute more liberally to the building fund. Cheerfully did the thousands of members comply with this request, awaiting confidently "the glad reunion upon the completion of the new edifice in Boston." [5]

When the Clerk of The Mother Church submitted his report at the Annual Meeting of June 13, 1905, the general import was the same: "Christian Scientists have contributed already for this grand and noble purpose," said the Clerk, "but let us not be unconsciously blind to the further needs of the building fund, in order to complete this great work, nor wait to be urged or to be shown the absolute necessity of giving." [6] Furthermore, it was pointed out that no member need consult the action of his neighbor in this respect nor be in the least concerned with how much individuals or churches had already contributed. Convincingly it was shown that giving to The Mother Church building fund was a matter of individual demonstration.

Also with the purpose of safeguarding the impersonal nature of the undertaking, it was understood that the Directors did not desire any special gifts from persons or groups of persons for the new church building. That is to say, no one should be permitted to offer, in lieu of money, any portion of the structure or any special feature of its decoration. In the Original Mother Church, for example, the organ was a thank offering from one of Mrs. Eddy's students whose invalid wife had been healed, the so-called "picture" windows were gifts of the students, and the children had contributed the furnishings for the Mother's Room. This time a clearer vision had revealed that it was nearer right for all to give their offerings into the one general fund; that all, again including

[5] *Miscellany*, p. 21.
[6] *Ibid.*, p. 22.

the building begins

the children, should give money to be used as the Directors deemed advisable. Thus was a double purpose achieved: the perfect homogeneity of the building in process of erection was assured, as well as the selflessness of the offerings which made its erection humanly possible.

problems with the design

What sort of building, then, was this new Mother Church Extension to be? Who had drawn its plans and who was to be its builder?

As early as December, 1902, Mrs. Eddy had let it be known that she desired Mr. E. Noyes Whitcomb, who was connected with a well-known and reliable firm of contractors, to act as the builder. Mr. Whitcomb did undertake the construction and proceed with it for a certain length of time; but while it was still in progress Mr. Whitcomb passed on, and until early in October of 1905 the work was carried on by his estate. Thereafter the masonry and other important contracts were placed with various well-established firms.

Mr. Charles Brigham of Boston was appointed architect and later the services of Mr. Solon S. Beman of Chicago were enlisted in an advisory capacity. Towards the close of the building operation, the firm of Brigham, Coveney and Bisbee was organized; and thereafter all the dealings of the Board of Directors were with this firm. Mr. Brigham held a position of note in his profession, having designed buildings of distinction in and near Boston. His was the old Art Museum building which Bostonians remember as a former adornment of Copley Square; his was also the rear addition to the Massachusetts State House on Beacon Hill.

As Mr. Brigham and Mr. Coveney set about the preparation of the drawings for the new structure, they found that theirs was no simple task. In the first place, the shape of the lot (as has already been pointed out) was both unusual and extremely difficult to adjust to any preconceived ideals of form and design. The architects must provide for an auditorium which would seat five thousand people, and they must erect it upon a lot which was both small and of a peculiar shape. At first it seemed to them that the thing could not be done. Hour after hour the two men worked, each over his own drawing board; day after day, they tested one plan, abandoned it, tried another. So many practically insuperable problems presented themselves that sometimes the two men were plunged in discouragement. In memory they harked back to all the mightiest and most beautiful structures of the world—buildings which rank among the art treasures of civilized man, buildings which are the common heritage of cultured men everywhere. Surely something of their beauty and majesty could be captured for embodiment in this future temple of a gloriously new and forward-looking land.

Perhaps the basilica of Saint Sophia at Constantinople offered a certain suggestion as to the form of the auditorium; then the dome of St. Peter's in Rome, it might be, or Brunelleschi's renowned dome on the cathedral in Florence was the inspiration for other features of the structure. Everything which lived in the memories of those two careful students of architecture was revived and tested as to its accord with the present requirements. Many such mental pictures were laid aside for further consideration; more were at once and definitely discarded; a few were accepted as including certain features which were desirable. But in the end it was not possible to say that The Mother Church Extension was like any other structure in the world; though it incorporated widely varying features pertaining to many structures. As the result of almost inexhaustible labors, at last inspiration came—inspiration which was the composite outcome of long contemplation of many styles belonging to many periods and realms. The Mother Church Extension could, in

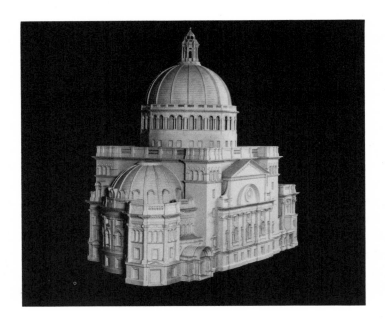

Architect's model for the Extension

the very nature of things, resemble no other single building. Never before had a church been required to fulfill the precise purpose for which this temple was designed.

During the architects' consideration of the great religious edifices of the East, it was in the Mosque of Ahmed I, in Constantinople, a conspicuous example of the type, that they found at last the plan motif, the use of which, combined with features from other sources, brought the solution long desired. Thus the germ of the idea which led to the outcome of the problem was Byzantine; but, as work on the plans progressed, distinctly Eastern features were little by little classicized. The domical ceilings of the auditorium indicate that the form of the structure required at least a suggestion of Eastern influence; but elsewhere the revived classical architecture of the Renaissance in Italy furnished the inspiration. And, withal, there was achieved an attribute which loomed important to Mrs. Eddy—the truly churchly character of the

112

building. She always wished a Christian Science church to be, as a whole and in every detail, unmistakably designed for religious worship. In common with others who express their tastes and inclinations naturally, Mrs. Eddy liked best the beautiful things which she knew and understood.

Since the Original Edifice was built, Mrs. Eddy had changed her feeling with regard to the "picture" windows. "Perhaps," she wrote to one member of The Christian Science Board of Directors in November, 1905, "you had better have a less number of picture windows, I think you had for there are so many in the first building. Please let Mr. Beman decide this question as well as all others relative to our Church extension." [1] There seems, too, to have been a general impression that all suspicion of symbolism was to be avoided; although, inadvertently, there did creep in here and there in the ornamentation two or three of the ancient classical designs. Those possessed of more than average perseverance and sharp vision may discover traces of such designs, but it would be a mistake to suppose that they have any significance whatever.

It was interesting that those four thousand wooden piles, to support the foundations, were driven in December, in winter weather—a circumstance then most unusual. But this was only one instance which went to prove that the erection of this edifice was not to be hedged about with the prescribed rules and limitations which so frequently attach themselves to ordinary building projects. One obstacle after another was met and overcome. For example, there was for a short time a little trouble over obtaining the permit to erect so high a building in that particular district of Boston. The first application for a permit was refused, but appeal of this decision was made, and in March, 1905, the needed permission was granted by the Building Department. As the digging for the foundations was done by hand, so was the placing of the enormous amount of cement concrete for the substructure, for the most part, accomplished by hand

[1] From the Historical Files of The Mother Church.

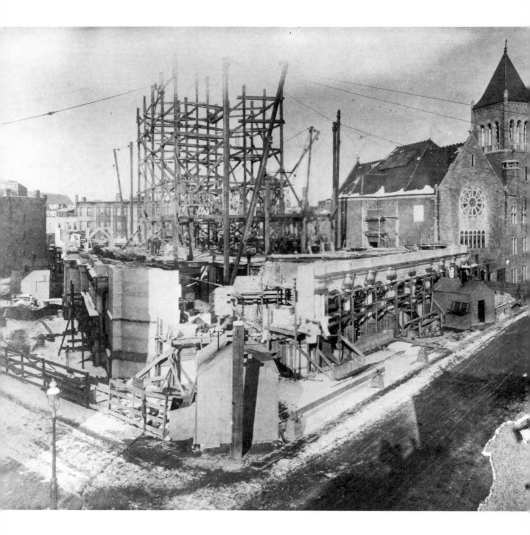

Construction of the triangular-shaped building begins

power—modern methods of mixing and pouring not having come into general use. Granite, quarried in Fitzwilliam, New Hampshire, Mrs. Eddy's native state, was chosen for the facing of walls and arcades of the architectural basement; while the marble to be used and carved for architraves, arcade capitals, and the tympana over doorways was quarried in Tennessee. The building of The Mother Church Extension was remarkable for the fact that more kinds of material, and with less duplication of parts, entered into its structure than may be found in most similar buildings.

Many who are familiar with the structure known as the Extension—many who wend their way there at least twice each week for the Sunday and Wednesday services—will be surprised to learn that the building does not display all the features which had taken shape in the minds of its architects.

For example, the problem of housing the chime of bells led to a plan to build an exterior single bell tower at the corner of Falmouth and St. Paul streets, adjacent to the front entrance of the Administration Building. The design underwent many alterations; but at one time the plan was entertained to build small dome turrets as well, designed to rise from the square corner porticoes and serve to break a too sudden transition from those stalwart corners to the dome. Again, one in a position to consult the architect's original plan is interested to note how much more the building, as then conceived, resembled an Eastern Mosque—an aspect accentuated by the campanile at the corner and by the smaller, slenderer dome turrets which were to rise towards the central dome. These features, as is well known today, were never finished for reasons which will presently be disclosed.

The delivery of beams for the campanile had begun on July 15, 1904, and continued in regular order and at considerable expense. Somewhat later the Board of Directors coincided with the opinion of the architects that it would be wise to eliminate the campanile as a second prominent feature and to use the cupola of the dome for the purpose for which the campanile was intended—namely, the housing of the chime of bells. For a while, the desirability of terminating both campanile and octagons with domical structures was considered; but finally it was concluded that it would be preferable to stop the structure at the level of the main cornice.

In this connection it is striking to reflect that the foundation of concrete locked with iron girders still stands, so that a tower could be erected upon that site at any time. The workmen had built up the campanile walls for quite a distance before the decision to omit that feature was made and the order given to desist. So it was finished off by a concrete roof arch, as seen today, and the architects contrived a decoration for the top of the octagon.

Thus it is evident how different is The Mother Church Extension today from the vision of it which its architects first caught. It is significant that the details of the building, making for beauty and for utility, unfolded slowly as the work proceeded; and that the Directors and the architects were at one in their vision of the fitness of the whole. As the necessary funds for the erection of the building were received when needed, so were all mental concepts of the finished structure developed at the right time in the thought of all concerned.

work accelerates

Again an editorial in the *Christian Science Sentinel* for November 25, 1905, reported that progress of the work on the Extension was proceeding satisfactorily; that there were then fifteen different trades represented by the army of workmen. The amazing thing was that, though all these kinds of work were in progress at the same time, the men did not obstruct each other's activities in the least. In order that not a single hour of the twenty-four should be lost, for a part of the period during which the structure was building the men worked in three shifts of eight hours each. It having been decided to dedicate the church in June, 1906, from August of 1905 the speed at which the work progressed was accelerated. Days, even hours, were reckoned with, calculations made meticulously, ingenuity and energy exercised without stint; and unremitting supervision of all work was maintained by the office of the architect.

From early in February of 1906, the interior became the scene of almost unbelievable activity. Large quantities of material, fabricated in many places, were being brought together by workmen of many trades; and they increased daily. An eyewitness described the auditorium of the future as "a veritable forest of wooden supports, crossing and recrossing to form the various stagings for the convenience of the workmen . . . . It is a wonder how the workmen themselves manage to move about through the maze."

The construction throughout the building, it may be recorded, was of the first class; the materials were simple, durable, and excellent, and neither cost nor effort was spared to make certain that they were put together in the most expert fashion. This fact, at least in part, accounts for the extraordinary freshness of The Mother Church Extension to this day. Little indication does it betray of the passing of the years since it was completed.

As to the material chosen for the exterior of the structure, it had been the first intention to use Tennessee marble; and only when it was found that such marble could not be procured promptly enough was the decision made to use Bedford limestone in the construction of the outside walls of the church.

In connection with the purchase of the Bedford stone, an interesting anecdote may be recalled. It so happened that one who was later a member of The Christian Science Board of Directors was at that time a director of the Cleveland Stone Company, of which the Indiana Quarries constituted a subsidiary. From that quarry in Indiana it had been decided that the Bedford limestone should be procured. This gentleman, on a day in the summer of 1905, by special request, joined a member of The Christian Science Board of Directors and Mr. Brigham, the architect, at Bedford, Indiana.

On the train it was observed that Mr. Brigham carried in his hand a small package of about the size of a letterhead and perhaps one inch thick. This small package Mr. Brigham kept constantly beside him; he would not put it down, neither would he explain its contents. When the three men met at Bedford, having deposited their luggage (all except the precious small package) at their lodgings, they went at once to the quarries. There the general superintendent conducted them about. At length they came to the best section of all, where on either side of the quarry ledge ran a railroad track bordered by large blocks of stone awaiting shipment. These blocks, each one containing about two hundred and fifty to three hundred and fifty cubic feet, were piled three or four blocks high for a considerable distance. It was an impressive sight.

After a little time, during which the four persons examined those great blocks of stone, Mr. Brigham suddenly began to unfold the wrappings of his package. When they were discarded, there was revealed a small piece of limestone which, compared with the quarried blocks along the railroad track, proved to be an exact counterpart. The three men were overjoyed; here was precisely the outcome hoped for.

Seeing their intense interest, the superintendent asked how much stone was needed, to which Mr. Brigham replied that the building would need about two hundred thousand cubic feet.

And the superintendent, thoroughly aroused now on his own part, continued: "Well, just look across the quarry opening at that big square block of unquarried stone. We have kept that for some special purpose, not knowing exactly what it was for; but there is the finest lot of stone in our quarry and it contains about two hundred thousand cubic feet. If you want that, I will reserve it for you."

By reason of its obvious suitability, the stone referred to was held until the definite order for it could be sent back to Bedford shortly after the return of the gentlemen to Boston. That written order called for any portion of two hundred thousand feet of Bedford stone which might be required for the completion of the structure of The Mother Church Extension. It was but one reassuring instance of the way in which the needs of the new structure were met without conscious planning on the part of anyone concerned; a comforting illustration of how "all things work together for good to them that love God," [1] when an upright purpose is pursued in a humble and obedient way.

It was proved possible for engineering work on the Extension to proceed throughout the winter, a circumstance by no means unusual today, but which was not so regarded at that date. And many observers were impressed by the continuance of unusually clement weather.

[1] Rom. 8:28.

119

work accelerates

Something has been said as to the materials used: that only the best were chosen and that all were expertly put together. In general, the interior structure is of the skeleton type, a frame of steel supporting and holding firmly in place all covering materials. The roof construction also is of steel. Little wood is used anywhere in the building, with the exception of the furniture and a portion of the frames of the doors. The walls, stairways, floors, and ceilings have steel frames, tile and cement construction. At this time steel structures were just coming into frequent use.

Great forethought was practiced with regard to the ordering and assembling of the materials. As a result, they were ready when needed. Everything was kept moving steadily, without a break; but enormous pains were taken that this should be so. Often a man from the office of the architect would journey to quarry or factory or foundry to make sure that there would be no delay; and the same man would follow the train on which materials were transported, to guard against breakdowns or other hindrances. Then, too, it became necessary most carefully to protect the materials after they had been assembled on the premises; for there was the realization of the great delay that would be caused, should any materials have to be replaced.

On the part of the workmen, in spite of some problems involving delays and minor strikes, there was an extraordinary sense of cooperation. On the whole, the work proceeded smoothly. Something which the men could not have defined held their allegiance, made them aware that the task on which they were engaged was no ordinary one. A person having the opportunity to visit the unfinished church by night would certainly have detected no diminution in activity. Parts of the rapidly rising structure would be in dense shadow, while other parts in which the work was going forward would be like vast shining pools of light. For many months, Mr. Charles C. Coveney, the architect's chief assistant, practically camped upon the premises, the better to watch everything which went forward there. Once, to be

The Extension rises

sure, there was a strike among the men. Pickets were one day lined up along the top of the fence to note who came and went; the matter was settled finally in court, but all the while the work went forward.

Some of the contracts were notable in the world of contractors. Take, for example, that of the many lighting fixtures. There was an intricate and a baffling problem. Plans were made, much discussion had to be entered into—so vast was the building to be lighted, so varied the positions and styles of fixture that were required. There was at one time involved discussion as to which firm should receive the contract. A day arrived when the matter had definitely to be settled without further delay. A committee, of which Mr. Ira O. Knapp was one, met in a small room in the Original Mother Church, early one winter morning. There those men remained until seven-thirty that evening, without food; and the weather was so bitterly cold that Mr. Knapp, huddled in his overcoat, spent all those hours seated as near as possible to a radiator. But the question was solved and the contract handed to a firm in New York City. No sacrifices were too great, no labors too arduous, to solve the endless tangle of problems which continued to present themselves. The church must be as near perfection as could be attained by human endeavor.

One of the most valuable of all the personal services rendered was that of the Rev. James J. Rome, a devoted student of Christian Science. He has told his own story with striking force and beauty in a letter which he sent to Mrs. Eddy, a letter of gratitude written after the Extension was completed. It seems that the Directors, needing someone to watch in the new structure at night, asked Mr. Rome if he would give his attention to this important task. It was required of him to be there each night, to watch and protect and further progress as best he could. Mr. Rome at once made this responsibility his chief concern. Night after night, during a period which stretched into weeks and then into months, he spent in the unfinished building, walking about, watching, standing, as he has recorded in his letter, under "the great dome, in the dark stillness of the night," and thinking, "What cannot God do?"

For a brief time, even Mr. Rome came under the prevalent fear that The Mother Church Extension would not be finished in time for the communion service and Annual Meeting of June, 1906. He has described graphically how he stumbled and groped amid a wilderness of stones and planks and heaps of plaster, struggling with the temptation to doubt that proper progress was being made. Then came light into his consciousness; he doubted no longer. "One feature about the work interested me," he has written. "I noticed that as soon as the workmen began to admit that the work could be done, everything seemed to move as by magic; the human mind was giving its consent. This taught me that I should be willing to let God work." [2] The workmen having complied with the expectation that the work on the church edifice would be finished on time, the outcome was as good as assured.

Always it was an important consideration that the flow of money should continually meet the requirements. Not always was it ready in the hands of the Board of Directors; it had to be asked for, the privilege of contributing presented over and over to the thought of the church members; but the money came when it was needed. Never was there any real question of whether or not there would be money enough to warrant the taking of a contemplated step. Instead, the consideration related to whether or not the proposed step or action was wisely justified.

[2] *Miscellany*, p. 61.

Mrs. Eddy's interest

During the erection of The Mother Church Extension, the details of its interior were guarded most carefully from the knowledge of the general public. At first a few persons were admitted, but later this privilege was found to be impracticable. There was, therefore, evidence both of idle curiosity and of genuine interest. Nevertheless, through the vigilance of the overseers who took charge by day, of Mr. Rome and others by night, all not directly concerned with the business of construction were excluded. Now and then the local newspapers would carry an article which discussed the progress of the work, with speculation as to the probable appearance of the finished building.

As a religion, Christian Science had known such amazing growth in forty years that already it required at the central point of its movement a church capable of seating five thousand persons. It can be readily understood that Mrs. Eddy herself, as Discoverer and Founder of Christian Science, was deeply concerned in the erection of the new Extension. While it is true that she did not visit it either during or after its erection, it is to be emphatically stated that she took an absorbing interest in its welfare and progress. Indeed, on March 26, 1904, she approved the floor plan of the Extension as later accepted, stating specifically that she considered the exterior aspect of the church beautiful.

Again and again came evidence of the keenness of her

watchfulness, evidence that she was aware of every step to be taken, supporting the progress of the work, guiding, warning, encouraging those engaged upon its construction. Earlier still, in January, 1904, she requested the Board of Directors to "retain the words at the entrance of my room in the [original] Mother Church, Rev. Mary B. Eddy's Room, the Children's Offering." [1] The inscription for the dedicatory tablet, on the outside of the Extension, was also her special care. "Be sure that the inscription on the new Mother Church is not placed over the door, such a situation suggests notices whereas the walls of an edifice suggest history or a dignified place for a record" [2]—this instruction was included in a letter which she forwarded to the Board of Directors.

As to numerous inscriptions which appear on the inside of The Mother Church Extension, Mrs. Eddy herself chose them. Visitors to Boston have wondered at the many wall inscriptions, remembering the steps which had been taken to limit the number and the diversity of inscriptions within the range of choice by the branch churches. By way of explanation, it will suffice to say that Mrs. Eddy selected them and understood their fitness in The Mother Church. Many, too, have noted that the familiar passage which appears on the large tablet at the right of the Readers' platform and over one of the side doors, differs in exact wording from the corresponding passage as found in the Christian Science textbook. [3] Again the simple and satisfying explanation is that Mrs. Eddy, with loving and inexhaustible forethought, rewrote that passage for its inscription upon the walls of the new church, sending it to the Board of Directors with the request that the new version, not that found in *Science and Health*, should be carved in the mellow stone. The same explanation applies to the other passages inscribed on the walls.

[1] From the Historical Files of The Mother Church.
[2] Ibid.
[3] See *Science and Health with Key to the Scriptures*, p. 270.

THIS EDIFICE ERECTED
ANNO DOMINI 1904
IS AN EXTENSION OF
THE FIRST CHURCH OF CHRIST
SCIENTIST
ERECTED ANNO DOMINI 1894
A TESTIMONIAL
TO OUR BELOVED TEACHER
THE REVEREND MARY BAKER EDDY
DISCOVERER AND FOUNDER
OF CHRISTIAN SCIENCE
AUTHOR OF ITS TEXT BOOK
SCIENCE AND HEALTH
WITH KEY TO THE SCRIPTURES
PRESIDENT OF THE
MASSACHUSETTS METAPHYSICAL COLLEGE
AND FIRST PASTOR
OF THIS DENOMINATION

Dedicatory tablet

Mrs. Eddy's interest

In sympathy and in thought, Mrs. Eddy must have been many times within the Extension, even if in the flesh she came no nearer to it than to drive one day in her carriage to a spot where she could see its great dome looming high against the blue sky. When in the spring of 1906, not long before the completion of the church, the Directors wrote to inform Mrs. Eddy that it had been unanimously resolved to make all seats in the Extension free, both on Sundays and on Wednesdays (except that pew reserved for Mrs. Eddy herself and one for each of the Directors), she sent this message in her own hand: "Beloved: I am pleased with the above." [4] Mrs. Eddy, of course, never occupied the pew which was formerly roped off and reserved for her use—which still bears the tablet with her name inscribed upon it—though guests of hers were occasionally ushered into seats there; neither for many years have the members of The Christian Science Board of Directors had special pews reserved for them.

Clearly, then, there is conclusive evidence that Mrs. Eddy's thoughts and interest were continuously engaged in the great task which her followers had in hand.

In the meantime, a vast company of laborers were devoting their time and attention to developing those precise details in which the public, both within and without the movement, displayed so much interest. The details, referred to, were legion. Just take, for example, the organ.

From his seat in the auditorium, a member of the congregation is confronted by rows of gilded pipes, filling the recesses above the Readers' platform at the east side of the building. He may suspect that there are many more pipes which he does not see; he hears, mysteriously, an occasional sound issuing from the base of the dome where he descries a perforation of the otherwise solid decorative design. Even though he be something of a musician, the likelihood is that he understands little of the construction of an organ.

The average layman, then, will wish to learn that this organ was made by a well-known Boston firm. The specifications

[4] From the Historical Files of The Mother Church.

The organ

were furnished by Mr. Albert F. Conant, then organist of The Mother Church, and by a distinguished Boston organist, Mr. B. J. Lang; organists who were organ architects also having been called in often to aid the builders. The average visitor will wish to know that, though this organ possessed in the beginning nearly five thousand pipes, only sixty-five of them are visible. The rear of the Original Church organ projects into the organ of the Extension, the two sets of pipes crowding each other closely for space. The display pipes extend approximately sixty feet across the front of the church.

When installing an organ, its correct placement is the consideration of chief importance. If it is possible to allow space between the top of the organ pipes and the ceiling, as exists in most cathedrals abroad, the instrument's beauty of tone is greatly enhanced. The circumstance permits the listener to hear the pure, direct tone as it comes, without interference, from the pipes. The tone is, therefore, clear and unmuffled in The Mother Church Extension; and moreover the ceiling and stone walls of the building make an ideal encasement for the tones of an organ.

This particular organ is suited both in quality and in size to the building which it graces. Its pure organ tone, or diapason quality, both in rich timbre and in brilliant mixtures, is outstanding and comparable to the foremost cathedral organs of Europe. The variety of tonal color, the solo stops of great beauty, and the modern mechanical devices for execution enable the organist to present to the best advantage modern compositions as well as the classics. And yet one may have but a slight understanding of the scope of this organ until he attends an Annual Meeting in The Mother Church Extension. At such a time, the auditorium being crowded, one experiences the full volume of the instrument; then its strength and grandeur come into play; then is this "king of instruments" truly heard.

In this church the echo organ has a peculiar mission. It is built in the ceiling, behind the grill work of the decoration, in front of and to the left of the main organ. Its position makes it available for customary antiphonal (or responsive) purposes; and also it is near enough to the rest of the organ to be played in ensemble with it. Here is installed a set of chimes or tubular metal bars; and, because of their unusual placement, visitors often inquire if these are not the same bells that they had heard when outside the church edifice. But the fact is that these bells are played from the console, or keyboard, of the organ itself.

As evidence of the continual desire to add to the beauty and harmony of The Mother Church edifice, one of the most interesting innovations was the modernization of the organ in 1928. At the time when other alterations and complete renovations were taking place in the auditorium, the organ was provided with an entirely new console embodying modern features. More than a thousand pipes, too, were added. The tonal range of the chime, located in the echo organ, was increased from twenty to twenty-five notes and several sets of modern string tones were incorporated in the general plan. Thirty registers in the organ were increased in compass from sixty-one to seventy-three notes, in keeping with more modern usage. Yet, although the tonal resources are more than adequate for the most enthusiastic congregational singing, there is seldom an impression of mere overwhelming noise. The organ is at all times distinguished by richness and variety, devoid of the necessity of the forcing of its tones.

the bells

To a person walking in Boston's Back Bay, in the vicinity of The Mother Church, it is no uncommon experience to observe a change of expression on the face of a passerby, a quick grateful glance upwards, a keen listening attitude. The simple explanation is that The Mother Church chime of bells has begun to peal. The sound brings joy both to Christian Scientists and to others who live in the neighborhood or else have cause to pass that way. Christian Scientists who live far away from Boston, who may perhaps have been longing for years to visit The Mother Church, often hear the bells before they actually see the edifice and so are indescribably comforted. Throughout untold generations one of the principal functions of bells has been to ring out glad tidings; and this service is performed by the bells of The Mother Church in a sense more literal, more deeply satisfying, than is true of other bells.

The bells which were installed in the tower of the Original Church were tubular. Had similar bells been placed at the great height above the street which was the necessary position of the bells in the Extension, they would have proved inadequate through lack of proper volume. Hence bells of the regular shape were desired. A representative of the Board of Directors was dispatched to hear and examine all the finest chimes of bells within a reasonable radius of Boston, thus to determine who should make the chime for The Mother Church Extension.

Among other notable bells, those hung in the tower of the Metropolitan Life Insurance Building in New York City were heard. Those four bells, lodged in their tower which rises to a height of six hundred and fifty feet, are said to hang higher above the ground than any other bells in the world. Their sound-carrying quality is remarkable, for they may be heard plainly for some twenty-eight miles, even out at sea beyond Sandy Hook. From the long-established firm which made the bells in the Metropolitan tower were finally ordered the bells for The Mother Church Extension.

The *ringing* of bells has, in many lands, been a calling handed down proudly from father to son; and, in the case of the firm in question, this rule has held true with regard to the *making* of bells. At the time referred to, the firm was composed of a father and three sons, whose forebears cast some of the first bells made in the United States. For several generations, the family has been making bells of all kinds: bells for churches and factories, bells for courthouses and for the towers of schools, bells for ships, bells for fire stations. Their

The bellringer's desk

bells are expertly made of honest materials; they are mounted in the most approved manner; they are fully warranted. Hence the bells were chosen with slow and deliberate care, one at a time, until as a result the chime is one of distinction.

Of course, the bells sound differently at different times. People have been known to declare that they needed tuning, that they were too sharp or too flat, too loud or too faint; while the fact is that it is practically impossible for these bells to be out of tune. It is not readily understood that external conditions alter their sound; that, for instance, as is an established fact, bells hung near water carry much farther than do other bells. Also that the position of the listener alters the case. Once a bell has been cast, the only cause which is likely to change its pitch is constant use. After many years, the clapper gradually wears a hollow at the point where it strikes and this may change somewhat the pitch of the bell. To remedy this, the bells can be turned so that the clapper shall strike in a new position. After such bells are forged, they cannot be tuned. Hence the supreme importance of having the bells right at the outset.

The bells

the bells

The chimer must mount to the platform from which the bells are played—198 steps from the street to the ringing platform, which is suspended about twenty feet above the inner dome or the apex of the auditorium. There are, in reality, three domes, the ringing platform being between the first and second. The bells, on the other hand, are in the lantern which tops the dome which is surmounted by a pineapple. That lantern is at an elevation of 224 feet above the street, to which one mounts to the bells by a series of iron staircases.

The chimer, man or woman—and to both have fallen the responsibility of playing The Mother Church chime—has, therefore, a climb before each service. Moreover, the bells peal on special occasions as well as on Christmas Eve and Christmas morning. On the day in 1918 when the Armistice was signed, it goes without saying that the bells of The Mother Church did their part to spread the glad news. But no person is required to play the bells when, three times each day, they precede the regular striking of the hours, by repeating the familiar Handel phrase which was written especially for bells. At seven o'clock in the morning, at noon, and at six o'clock in the evening, that Handel phrase is reproduced by clock control.

It may, in this connection, be of interest to record that the hymns which are played before a Sunday service in The Mother Church are always chosen with careful reference to the subject of that day's Lesson-Sermon, though they are not invariably the precise hymns which will be sung at that service. Not all hymns can be played on the bells, some having too great a range. It is usual to play about nine hymns before a service, the playing of the bells continuing for twenty to twenty-two minutes or until the playing of the organ begins within the auditorium.

In former days, many an eager visitor has, with the permission of the Board of Directors and by courtesy of the chimer, mounted to the ringing platform; though for some persons the climb is something of an ordeal. Nevertheless,

the bells

many have struggled with and overcome their aversion to the steep ascent of the iron stairs or their fear of looking off from high places. This fact is movingly illustrated by the following incident:

One Sunday morning a woman presented herself at the church with her two children, who greatly desired to see the bells played. Permission had been given and they set out with the chimer. The mother and the little girl ascended joyfully and easily, but for the boy it seemed more difficult as he was slightly lame. He went on more slowly, but he went steadily until the party arrived at the still more precipitous iron stair which finishes the ascent.

At the sight of that final stair, the little boy quailed and his mother, filled with apprehension for his safety, quickly told him that he must go no farther. For him it would not be prudent. The boy was deeply disappointed; he had heard the bells again and again, but he had never seen them played. However, he could do nothing but obey his mother, who stayed behind, too, to comfort him, while the chimer and the little girl continued on their way. There was no time to be lost in argument.

Several beautiful hymns had rung out upon the Sunday morning quiet, when the chimer began to play the one which asks: "Why is thy faith in God's great love so small?" Several times she went over it, each time with what seemed more strength and conviction; it was almost as if the uplifting words were being sung to the accompaniment. Suddenly the chimer was aware of another presence on the ringing platform than that of the little girl who stood beside her, watching. There stood the lad, with his mother close behind him on the iron stair. Their faces were aglow. The chiming of that hymn had dispelled their fears.

Afterwards the little boy protested with shining eyes: "Why, Mother, I wouldn't for anything in the world have missed seeing those bells played."

The bells are twelve in number, ranging in weight from

three hundred and fifty pounds to two tons. Considerable strength is required to play them, a task which is accomplished with both hands and feet. To quote the words which have come with authority from the makers, "All of the bells, with the exception of the tenor, or largest, which is mounted in the full manner of a church bell, so that it can be rung independently of the others, as occasion may require, are suspended in stationary form from a framework, suited to the tower, and are sounded by means of chains and rods leading from the clappers and passing through pulleys to the position of the ringer, where they are attached by movable straps to the manuals, in the form of levers, which are operated by a single player."

In an article which appeared in the issue of the *Christian Science Sentinel*, dated June 7, 1930, attention was called to the fact that Mrs. Eddy was extremely fond of bells. When The Mother Church was built, Mrs. Eddy made the request that bells be installed therein; and she also provided them for First Church of Christ, Scientist, in Concord, New Hampshire. And when the Directors wrote Mrs. Eddy that their plan was to inscribe upon the major or tenor bell of the chime: "The First Church of Christ, Scientist," Mrs. Eddy's reply proposed the following amplified inscription:

> The First Church of Christ, Scientist
> in Boston, Massachusetts
> 1906
> Founded on Love

This inscription appears on the great tenor bell, precisely as she designated.

the final touches

It is a well-known fact that Christian Scientists the world over do not dedicate their churches until they are wholly paid for. The Extension of The Mother Church involved, of course, no departure from this rule. At the Annual Meeting of June 1, 1905, Mr. Stephen A. Chase, the Treasurer, reported that the sum of $1,108,539.51 was still needed to complete the pledge taken in June, 1902, for the raising of two million dollars. Later in that year an editorial in the *Christian Science Sentinel* for November 25th notified the church members that the work on the edifice was proceeding rapidly; and it closed by proposing that the coming Thanksgiving season would be a suitable one in which to complete the building fund, thus "making a special effort . . . to dispose fully and finally of this feature of the demonstration." [1]

Meanwhile doubts persisted in the minds of many as to the probability of the edifice being finished on the day of the coming Annual Meeting, June 10, 1906. Mr. Rome, who acted so faithfully as watchman in the new auditorium, has admitted that he harbored fears. The workmen now carried on in three shifts, throughout the night as well as the day; on one holiday which occurred during the last weeks before the church was finished, by special arrangement, all the men continued their work as usual. The interior of the great structure was still a busy hive, by natural light during the

[1] *Miscellany,* p. 25.

137

day and by the light of many electric lamps during the night. Manpower had been tremendously accelerated; and it is interesting to learn that it required fifty men by day and fifty men by night for the one task of setting the pews in place.

Nevertheless, many felt that the dedication would have to be postponed; others that the ceremony should be held at the stated time, no matter what stage of development the edifice had reached. Mrs. Eddy first expressed her desire with regard to the dedication in a letter to Mr. William B. Johnson, Clerk of The Mother Church, as follows: "In my prayer it has come to me: Do not have The Mother Church dedicated until it is completely finished outside and inside. I can see the wisdom of this, and the directors will see it if they follow this direction." [2] Later the day came when she withdrew what she had said and, in view of "the feeling . . . against postponing the dedication of our Church till it is finished throughout and paid for," [3] stated that, even if a few comparatively unimportant details should remain incomplete, the building was to be dedicated at the regular June Annual Meeting. Mrs. Eddy had seen more clearly than others the mental conflict which would ensue, were the church not completed and paid for before the dedication. In the end, she and her followers wrought so well that the goal was beautifully realized; the Extension of The Mother Church was ready to serve its purpose, although incomplete in some matters of ornamental finish, and the money was in hand to meet all ensuing costs, before the first Sunday in June, 1906.

There were many dramatic moments during those last weeks, while the Extension was receiving the final touches, just as there had been earlier when men still labored upon the exterior of the building—when, for example, one of the workmen who greatly desired to place the last stone on the building, but said nothing about his desire, was suddenly accorded that great privilege, upon succeeding after a

[2] From the Historical Files of The Mother Church.
[3] *Ibid.*

138

struggle of many years in overcoming the habit of smoking. Many such experiences have, unquestionably, gone unrecorded; but each one of which we are aware brings a quickened sense of gratitude and of inspiration.

Perhaps one of the most arresting of the stories related to the testing of the acoustics in the auditorium. This was done by one of the architects and a member of The Christian Science Board of Directors. It had not yet been possible to attempt the testing of the acoustics, because of the steel trestle which still remained; but the instant was approaching when these men would know how successful had been the solution of the difficult problem of the acoustics in this auditorium.

They stood side by side on the Readers' platform, watching the large trestle come down, section by section. From moment to moment, the aspect of the auditorium was changing, becoming more impressive. Finally the auditorium with its seven balconies and its dome was revealed without obstruction. There the two men stood, momentarily silenced. For, no matter how accustomed to the surroundings, each person who entered the church auditorium experienced his own fresh shock of surprise and wonder.

Then, pulling himself together, the architect descended from the platform and walked to the rear of the church; and, arrived there, he spoke in a normal, unexcited, unstrained voice. The man who stood on the platform heard him easily and, speaking in his own accustomed tones, was audible at the rear of the church. It had been proved that the acoustics of The Mother Church Extension would be remarkably satisfactory.

It is given, perhaps, to few persons to stand as did those two men on the Readers' platform. Hence it may not always be realized that, though some members of the congregation are seated far away on the edge of the auditorium and others in remote corners of the balconies—though they number on occasions in the neighborhood of five thousand—yet from the Readers' platform they do not seem far away, but close.

Thereafter certain details of the interior began rapidly to

The auditorium awaits services

shape themselves. Anyone whose business took him within the great auditorium might have gained some proper impression of its expanse, topped by the dome, eighty-two feet in diameter, which including the cupola rises to a height of 224 feet, supported on four arches which spring from giant stone piers—an auditorium containing twenty-five thousand square feet of floor space. A visitor might have admired the foreign marble of the Readers' platform, the soft gray-white of the Bedford stone, and the pews, which are of San Domingo mahogany. It was possible by this time to grasp some idea of the dimensions of the foyer on the ground floor, capable of permitting a large number of persons to move about freely; of the facilities of a cloakroom which would care for three thousand wraps; of the Sunday School room and offices for the Board of Directors.

Within the Extension edifice, space had become a willing servant, harnessed to fulfill the purposes of Mind.

dedication day

Mrs. Eddy had, as always, expressed the thought which was uppermost in the minds of her followers when, on April 8, 1906, she wrote: "I cannot be present *in propria persona* at our annual communion and the dedication in June next of The Mother Church of Christ, Scientist. But I shall be with my blessed church 'in spirit and in truth.' I have faith in the givers and in the builders of this church edifice,—admiration for and faith in the grandeur and sublimity of this superb superstructure, wherein all vanity of victory disappears and the glory of divinity appears in all its promise." [1]

On June 2, 1906, precisely eight days before the dedication services were to take place, came the next rejoicing. It was then that Mr. Chase, the Treasurer, made the following announcement: "The contributors to the building fund for the extension of The Mother Church, The First Church of Christ, Scientist, in Boston, Mass., are hereby notified that sufficient funds have been received for the completion of the church building, and the friends are requested to send no more money to this fund." [2] It was the complete assurance that the pledge for the raising of two million dollars, given so long ago as on the day of the Annual Meeting in June, 1902, had been triumphantly made good.

An editorial in the *Christian Science Sentinel* for June 2, 1906, gratefully alluded to this spiritual victory and said: "The

[1] *Miscellany*, p. 25.
[2] *Ibid.*, p. 27.

142

treasurer's books will show the dollars and cents received by him, but they can give no more than a hint of the unselfish efforts, and in many instances the loving self-sacrifice, of those who have given so generously to the building of this church. Suffice it to say, however, that the giving to this fund has stimulated those gentle qualities which mark the true Christian, and its influence upon the lives of thousands has been of immense value to them." [3]

As for the outside world—the comment made in print and by word of mouth—no one fact aroused such astonishment as this announcement that the Christian Scientists were dedicating their church, which had cost two million dollars, free of debt. Probably, to the Christian Scientists themselves, this was the feature least worthy of comment. For such had been their intent from the start. They had known that it would be so.

The story of that Sunday of June 10, 1906, which was both communion Sunday and the Sunday of the dedication, has been told and retold many times. Newspapers heralded it far and wide, photographs too depicted it vividly; and those who were present have never wearied of rehearsing their reminiscences, whether one refers to distinguished visitors from abroad or to a gentleman who came from his home in the suburbs to act as usher. "There were six services that day and I ushered at all of them," so he has written. "I left home at five o'clock in the morning and did not return until ten o'clock at night." Similar recollections flood the consciousness of all who participated in events of that inspiring day.

Boston, quite apart from any sense of denomination, opened its doors and its heart to the visitors. No city could have remained unresponsive in the presence of such thousands, all good-natured, patient, radiantly happy. Ships and special trains and extra sections attached to regular trains brought them to the city which, since the year when Mrs. Eddy moved there from Lynn, has continued to be the headquarters of the Christian Science movement. Those who

[3] *Miscellany,* p. 28.

Inside the Extension

Inside the Extension

145

were strange to Boston, as well as those who were not, found their way promptly to Horticultural Hall, at the corner of Huntington and Massachusetts Avenues, which had been designated as meeting place for the visiting throngs. Horticultural Hall was scarcely recognizable. It had become a reception office, an information bureau, a post office, a bureau of railroad information, and an agency for the renting of rooms in hotels and lodging houses; it offered both telephone and telegraph facilities. Once merged in the throngs which surged within its four brick walls, no one wished to leave. The place was aglow with the enthusiasm, the buoyancy, the rejoicing, and the gratitude of all those happy people, many of whom had undergone positive hardship and sacrifice of material things even to be there at all.

When Sunday dawned, it was greeted by the pealing of those new church bells which were to summon the throngs to attend the six services held within The Mother Church Extension. It was estimated that the services were attended by more than thirty thousand people. At six o'clock in the morning, the bells first rang out and, when seven-thirty came and with it the hour for the first service, hundreds of people were turned away. But how patiently they awaited their turns at the identical five services which followed, one of them—that at noon—being especially for the children. One woman, who spent a long time in the crowd outside one of the entrances, hopeful of being admitted for the next service, has left the following impression of that morning: "On the day of the dedication we were out at five o'clock in the morning, standing waiting for the church doors to open at seven o'clock. . . . What can I say of the dedication service? Everything has already been said. The wonder of hearing our Leader's message read, and of being among those who sent her a message, the singing of the hymns—all the stars singing together—and then the Lord's Prayer. I had never heard anything like it; it seemed to be said with one enormous voice, and I remembered how 'some said it thundered.' "

As a Boston newspaper expressed it: "When these people

Dedication Sunday

dedication day

enter this new cathedral or temple which has been in process of construction, they will find themselves in one of the most imposing church edifices in the country—yes, in the world. For in its interior architecture it is different from any other church in the world. In fact, nearly all the traditions of church interior architecture have been set aside in this temple, for here are neither nave, aisles, nor transept—just one vast auditorium which will seat exactly five thousand and twelve people on floor and galleries, and seat them comfortably." [4]

What were the precise feelings of the Christian Scientists who, on that day of rejoicing, entered The Mother Church Extension, it would be possible to describe in a thousand ways. Each heart alone responded in its individual and spontaneous manner. Perhaps, with many, there was at first a sense of breathless awe, then a quiet feeling of coolness and vastness for one coming in from the brilliant hot June sunshine without. It seemed that the building was too tremendous to see across, too lofty to permit the eye to soar as high as the top of the dome. All sorts of people were there, sitting in closely packed reverent rows, listening, watching, wondering. There were humble people and people richly dressed; there was even an Indian prince with his wife in native costume hung with pearls. There were elderly people, full of grateful remembrance; there were young people, alight with courage and with idealism. Such singing of the hymns, especially Mrs. Eddy's "Shepherd, show me how to go"; such responsive reading; such a surging unison of voices in repetition of the Lord's Prayer—all from the five thousand persons who had knelt there in silent communion. To record these memories in cold words is to impart a feeble impression of the actuality.

As for the Wednesday evening testimony meeting which followed the dedication Sunday, attendance overflowed from the new auditorium into the vestry of the Extension, into the Original Mother Church and its vestry, into seven large halls

[4] *Miscellany*, p. 71.

in the vicinity. Even then there were hundreds waiting vainly in the street, so great were the numbers of those who desired to share the expressions of gratitude. If proofs of the efficacy of the teachings of Christian Science had been lacking until that evening, they were then overwhelmingly supplied; for the healings reported included practically every known disease, to say nothing of the banishment of darkness and sadness, loneliness and failure.

Any lingering boastfulness in the hearts of her followers—any pride of place or of power or of achievement—had been effectually rebuked as they listened to the inspired words in the Dedicatory Message by their Leader, Mrs. Eddy: "We cannot serve two masters. Do we love God supremely? Are we honest, just, faithful? Are we true to ourselves? 'God is not mocked: for whatsoever a man soweth, that shall he also reap.' To abide in our unselfed better self is to be done forever with the sins of the flesh, the wrongs of human life, the tempter and temptation, the smile and deceit of damnation. When we have overcome sin in all its forms, men may revile us and despitefully use us, and we shall rejoice, 'for great is [our] reward in heaven.' " [5]

The Mother Church Extension was finished. Now Christian Scientists were offered the opportunity of progressing to yet more important, more significant proofs of God's power. So much had been clearly shown—that the "excelsior extension" of The Mother Church of Christ, Scientist, is its crown. But beyond that material symbol Mrs. Eddy pointed higher and still higher to mounts of purity which would assuredly be achieved through the demonstration of regeneration in the individual character. "Its crowning ultimate," she added in the closing lines of her Dedicatory Message, "rises to a mental monument, a superstructure high above the work of men's hands, even the outcome of their hearts, giving to the material a spiritual significance—the speed, beauty, and achievements of goodness." [6]

[5] *Miscellany*, p. 6.
[6] *Ibid.*

149

The Portico

the portico

A handsome new portico entrance to the Extension of The Mother Church was completed in 1975. It was the culmination of a comprehensive plan which opened up the area surrounding the Church and added several new buildings, retaining the focus on the Original Mother Church and its domed Extension.

In its plan, the architectural firm of I. M. Pei integrated the Church edifices and The Christian Science Publishing Society with three new structures: the slender 28-story Administration Building, the five-story Colonnade, and a quarter-round Sunday School. An open parklike setting—flower beds, linden trees, and a 670-foot reflecting pool, connected by brick walkways—complements and links the buildings.

With stone and glass fitted in graceful symmetry atop a strong foundation, the portico is a striking entrance—an invitation to visitors from around the world. Ten 42-foot Indiana limestone columns form the portico's classic half-rotunda. Its columns, hand-carved to match the details of the Extension, exemplify old-world stonework craftsmanship rarely called for in buildings today.

Impressive as these buildings are, they do not of themselves constitute the Church of Christ, Scientist, whose true

The Sunday School building
To the left—the portico under construction

entity was aptly described by Archibald McLellan on the completion of the Extension in 1906:

"The significance of this building is not to be found in the material structure, but in the lives of those who, under the consecrated leadership of Mrs. Eddy, and following her example, are doing the works which Jesus said should mark the lives of his followers. It stands as the visible symbol of a religion which heals the sick and reforms the sinful as our Master healed and reformed them. It proclaims to the world that Jesus' gospel was for all times and for all men; that it is as effective to-day as it was when he preached the Word of God to the multitudes in Judea and healed them of their diseases and their sins." [1]

[1] *Christian Science Sentinel*, June 9, 1906, and *The First Church of Christ, Scientist, and Miscellany*, p. 28.

letters from Mary Baker Eddy to Joseph Armstrong

(published by permission)

Concord, N.H., . . .

Give this [manuscript] to Miss———— to make it perfectly grammatical. I have not the time to read it all and it needs careful examination.

It [your manuscript] is prosaic in description, but to builders may prove interesting. Your detailed account is wonderful because of many things, your moral well drawn.

M. B. Eddy

N.B. Uniformity must be preserved in the title you mainly give to me.

You may insert my letters that you have chosen.
M. B. E.

Pleasant View
Concord, N.H., June 5, 1897
My beloved Student:
I thank you for the interesting, finely gotten-up volume—"The Mother Church." I enclose check for one dozen, in cloth. I want them to give away to people that the book will interest. Again thanking you more than all, for your faithful performance of your duties to which you alone were appointed by me in building The Mother Church.

To read the dear book is with feelings of an old soldier to fight anew the old battles.

With love, mother,
Mary Baker Eddy.

N.B. Please fill out the check. I leave it blank for you to add the price on one dozen of "The Mother Church," in cloth.

inscriptions on the walls of
The Mother Church Extension

Citations from the Bible and writings of Mary Baker Eddy inscribed on the walls of The Mother Church Extension

Foyer Stairway Landing

Verily, verily, I say unto you, He that heareth my word, and believeth on him that sent me, hath everlasting life, and shall not come into condemnation; but is passed from death unto life.

Christ Jesus

When we learn that sickness cannot kill us and that we are not saved from sin or sickness by death, this understanding will quicken us into newness of life. It will master either a desire to die or a dread of the grave, and thus destroy the great fear that besets mortal existence.

Mrs. Eddy

Left of Platform

He shall give you another Comforter, that he may abide with you for ever; Even the Spirit of truth; whom the world cannot receive, because it seeth him not . . . but ye know him; for he dwelleth with you.

Christ Jesus

inscriptions

Right of Platform

If sin makes sinners, Truth and Love can unmake them. If a sense of disease produces suffering, and a sense of ease antidotes it, disease is mental. Hence the fact in Christian Science that the human mind alone suffers, and the divine Mind alone heals it.

Mrs. Eddy

Over Platform

Preach the word; be instant in season, out of season; reprove, rebuke, exhort with all longsuffering and doctrine.

Paul

When error confronts you, withhold not the rebuke or explanation which destroys it. Never breathe an immoral atmosphere, unless in the attempt to purify it.

Mrs. Eddy

Under Right Balcony
First from Platform

One God and Father of all, who is above all, and through all, and in you all.

Paul

The First Commandment of the Hebrew Decalogue demonstrates Christian Science, the tri-unity of God, Spirit, Mind; and it signifies that man shall have no other spirit or mind but God, eternal good, and that all men shall be of one mind.

Mrs. Eddy

Second from Platform

All things were made by Him; and without Him was not anything made that was made.

John

inscriptions

Spirit, God, has created all in and of Himself, Spirit, the Aeon or Word of God. Spirit is the only substance, the invisible and indivisible God. Things spiritual and eternal are substantial. Things material and temporal are insubstantial.
Mrs. Eddy

Over Left Rear Door

And other sheep I have, which are not of this fold: them also I must bring, and they shall hear my voice; and there shall be one fold, and one shepherd.
Christ Jesus

Over Right Rear Door

Christ's Christianity is the chain of scientific being reappearing in all ages, maintaining the obvious correspondence with the Scriptures, and uniting all periods in the design of God.
Mrs. Eddy

Under Center Balcony

Left

He that loveth father or mother more than me is not worthy of me: and he that loveth son or daughter more than me is not worthy of me: and he that taketh not his cross, and followeth after me, is not worthy of me.
Christ Jesus

We are Christian Scientists only as we quit our reliance upon material things and grasp the spiritual. We are not Christian Scientists until we leave all for Christ.
Mrs. Eddy

inscriptions

Right

If we confess our sins, He is faithful and just to forgive us our sins, and to cleanse us from all unrighteousness. If we say that we have not sinned, we make Him a liar, and His word is not in us.

John

We acknowledge God's forgiveness of sin in the destruction of sin, and the spiritual understanding that evil is unreal, hence not eternal. But the belief in sin is punished so long as it lasts.

Mrs. Eddy

Under Left Balcony

Take no thought for your life, what ye shall eat.

Christ Jesus

The primitive custom of taking less thought about food gave the gospel a chance to be seen in its glorious effects upon the body. When the mechanism of the human mind gives place to the divine Mind, sin, disease and death will lose their foothold.

Mrs. Eddy

Over Third Center Balcony

Glory to God in the highest, and on earth peace, good will toward men.

Luke

To-day the healing power of Truth is widely demonstrated as an immanent, eternal Science. Its coming, as was promised by the Master, is for its establishment as a permanent dispensation. The mission of Christian Science now, as in the earlier demonstration thereof, is not one of physical healing only, but to attest the reality of its higher mission, namely the power of Christ, Truth, to take away the sins of the world.

Mrs. Eddy

inscriptions

In your patience possess ye your souls.
Christ Jesus

Like the great Exemplar, the healer should speak to disease as one having authority over it, leaving Soul to master the false evidence of the corporeal senses and assert its claims over mortality and sickness.
Mrs. Eddy

Over Check Room

Let this mind be in you, which was also in Christ Jesus: who, being in the form of God, thought it not robbery to be equal with God.
Paul

The same "Mind . . . which was also in Christ Jesus" must accompany the letter of Christian Science to heal the sick and repeat the ancient demonstrations of prophets and apostles. That those wonders are not more commonly repeated to-day arises not so much from lack of desire as from lack of spiritual growth.
Mrs. Eddy

Blessed are the pure in heart: for they shall see God.
Christ Jesus

Christian Science demonstrates that none but the pure in heart can see God. In proportion to his purity is man perfect; and perfection is the order of celestial being, which demonstrates life in Christ, its spiritual ideal.
Mrs. Eddy

We then, as workers together with him, beseech you also that ye receive not the grace of God in vain. For he saith, I have heard thee in a time accepted, and in the day of salvation have I succoured thee: behold, now is the accepted time; behold, now is the day of salvation.
Paul

inscriptions

If the Scientist reaches his patient through divine Love, he will accomplish the healing work at one visit, and the disease will vanish into its native nothingness like dew before the morning sunshine.

Mrs. Eddy

Corridor Adjoining Original Church

These signs shall follow them that believe; In my name shall they cast out devils; they shall speak with new tongues; they shall take up serpents; and if they drink any deadly thing, it shall not hurt them.

Christ Jesus

Jesus' promise was perpetual. Had it been given only to His immediate disciples, the Scriptural passage would read you not they. The purpose of his great life-work extends through time and touches universal humanity. Its Principle is infinite, extending beyond the pale of a single period or a limited following.

Mrs. Eddy

There is no fear in love; but perfect love casteth out fear.

John

When God bade Moses cast down his rod and it became a serpent, he fled before it; but God bade him handle the serpent; then his fear departed. And God said: "If they will not believe thee, neither hearken to the . . . first sign, they will believe . . . the latter." And so it was when the Science of being was demonstrated by Jesus, who taught his students how to heal the sick and cast out evils in proof of the supremacy of Mind.

Mrs. Eddy

Believe me that I am in the Father, and the Father in me: or else believe me for the very works' sake. Verily, Verily, I say unto you, He that believeth on me, the works that I do shall he do also.

Christ Jesus

inscriptions

Hold perpetually this thought: that it is the spiritual idea, the Holy Ghost or Christ, which enables you to demonstrate with scientific certainty the rule of healing, based upon its divine Principle, Love, underlying, overlying and encompassing all true being.

Mrs. Eddy

Sunday School Room

I am the resurrection, and the life: he that believeth in me, though he were dead, yet shall he live: and whosoever liveth and believeth in me shall never die.

Christ Jesus

He who perceives the true idea of Life loses his belief in death. He who has the right idea of good loses faith in evil, and by reason of this is being ushered into the undying realities of Spirit. Such a one abideth in Life,—life obtained not of the body, incapable of supporting life, but of Truth, developing its own immortal idea.

Mrs. Eddy

St. Paul Street Corridor

Wherefore God also hath highly exalted him, and given him a name which is above every name: that at the name of Jesus every knee should bow, of things in heaven, and things in earth, and things under the earth; and that every tongue should confess that Jesus Christ is Lord, to the glory of God the Father.

Paul

We acknowledge and adore one supreme and infinite God: we acknowledge His Son, one Christ; the Holy Ghost or divine Comforter; and man as His image and likeness.

Mrs. Eddy

index

The page numbers for quotations are printed in *italics,* and those for illustrations in **boldface.**

index

The page numbers for quotations are printed in *italics,* and those for illustrations in **boldface.**

index

The page numbers for quotations are printed in *italics,* and those for illustrations in **boldface.**

Moses, 24, 79, *81, 84*
Mother Church, The, by Joseph
    Armstrong, 106
Mother's Room, 28, 40, 63–69, *65,* **68,** 76

Neal, James A., 18–19, 76
No and Yes by Mrs. Eddy, 18
"Now and Then" by Mrs. Eddy, 102

Obstacles overcome, *see* Christian
    Science Board of Directors,
    obstacles overcome by
Organ, 42–43, 127–30, **128, 140**

Pastor, impersonal, 62, 70
Paul, *7, 21, 36, 63, 85, 161, 164, 166*
Pei, I. M., 153
Pews, 76–77, 127, 138

Retrospection and Introspection by
    Mrs. Eddy, 18
Rome, Rev. James J., 122–23, 124, 137
Rudimental Divine Science by Mrs. Eddy,
    18

Saint John, *see* John
Saint Paul, *see* Paul
Science and Health with Key to the Scriptures
    by Mrs. Eddy, 17, 42, 45, 46, 61, 67, 69,
    70, 106, 125
Site, 7, 8, 11, 96–97, 100–1, **104,** 105–6,
    110–11, 153
Stained glass windows, *see* Windows

Trustees, Board of, 7, 8, 63, 82

Unity of Good by Mrs. Eddy, 18

Watchmen, 18–19, 122–23, 124
Whitcomb, E. Noyes, 106, 110
Williams, Ella E., 106
Whittier, John Greenleaf, 69
Windows, stained glass, 25, 43–62,
    47–59, 67, 113
Workers, relations among, with, 23,
    36–41, 74, 117, 120–22